Every *Child* Needs a *Praying Mom*

Every *Child* Needs a *Praying Mom*

Fern Nichols

with
Janet Kobobel Grant

Founder and President of **MOMS IN TOUCH INTERNATIONAL**

ZONDERVAN™

GRAND RAPIDS, MICHIGAN 49530 USA

ZONDERVAN™

Every Child Needs a Praying Mom
Copyright © 2003 by Fern Nichols

This title is also available as a Zondervan audio product.

Requests for information should be addressed to:
Zondervan, *Grand Rapids, Michigan 49530*

ISBN 0-310-24584-2

Published in association with the literary agency of Ann Spangler and Company, 1420 Pontiac Road S.E., Grand Rapids, MI 49506.

Interior design by Susan Ambs

Printed in the United States of America

To my beloved husband,
Rle, my lifelong partner and friend.
Your prayers and loving support are treasured in my heart.

To my children, Ty, Troy, Travis, and Trisha.
Each of you has written page after page upon my heart
of God's faithfulness and loving-kindness.
I'm honored beyond words that I'm your mom.

And I'm abundantly blessed that God has given me
three beautiful, godly "daughters-in-love," Patti, Bonnie, and Tara.

And to my mom, for teaching me to pray.
I pray this book will be a legacy of God's power through prayer
to each succeeding generation of our family
and the family of God.

"Let this be written for a future generation,
that a people not yet created may praise the LORD"
(Psalm 102:18).

Contents

Foreword by Evelyn Christenson

One of the greatest miracles of God is His calling of single individuals to do gargantuan jobs for Him. God sees in these people what the Christian world may not yet recognize—that person's potential leadership, perseverance, sacrifice, and spiritual power. The Billy Grahams and the Mother Teresas of the world are such people—and so is Fern Nichols.

God saw multitudes of children in desperate need of prayer, and He saw Fern with her burning passion to pray for her own children as they faced peer pressure, classroom teaching contrary to their beliefs, and role models that challenged their lifestyle and faith in Jesus. Enlisting a few moms to pray with her, Fern's passion suddenly became a calling—from God Himself—that *every child needs a praying mom*. It was God's call for Fern to inspire and organize other moms to pray for their children—and God led this call to a ministry that exploded from the starting block to an amazing 150,000 moms praying in groups every single week.

My first memory of Fern is as a bubbly young mom with tireless passion for her fledgling organization seeking advice about corporate prayer. As we have become close personal and spiritual friends, I've watched her unquenchable passion turn into a single-minded lifestyle with the goal of giving every child the praying mom he or she needs—and deserves.

Are *you* reading this book because you too have a burning desire for God to protect your children from the evils vying for their minds and bodies through drugs, violence, and false teachings? Are you saying, "I'm too insignificant, unimportant for God to use *my* prayers?" *Never underestimate the power of one person's prayers—including your own!*

In this book Fern takes you personally on her journey of becoming a powerful pray-er. Her practical tools woven throughout the book show how you too can become a biblically accurate intercessor. Brimming with awesome true illustrations, this book will continuously propel you to trust what God will do when you have the courage to pray.

Fern will help you with answers to puzzling questions such as: How do I remain a confident pray-er even when God doesn't seem to be answering? How is Satan trying to hinder me from praying? How do I overcome the things that keep me from actually praying? Which Scriptures are, or are not, for everybody to pray? Does God send angels to answer my prayers? Is prayer necessary in Christian schools? How can I enlist teachers as pray-ers? And how can I cover in prayer the kids in my children's school who do not have a praying mom?

Fern's four steps explain in depth what to do in your prayer time, including why your most important prayer is for others' salvation: *praise* because of God's attributes, *confession* so you will have prayer power, *thanksgiving* "in" not "for" all things, and *intercession*.

This is one of the most uplifting books I've ever read. Page by page it pulled me ever closer to Jesus who loved all the children—and admonished His disciples to permit the little children to come to Him.

As I carefully read this manuscript, my whole being was engulfed with an unusual spiritual warmth and hope in the biblical assurance that God is still on His throne and *will* rescue our children—if we pray.

This book should not be lightly scanned but prayerfully studied with the same burning passion that God gave Fern. *Laboring, weeping, persevering, believing.* Study this book until you have applied its teachings—until you are transformed as a pray-er—until God is also producing miracles as you pray—until God answers each of your prayers in His way, in His time, and for His reasons—but always for the good of your child. *That's what a praying mom is.*

Introduction:
The Birth of a Prayer Movement

Growing up, all I wanted was to be a mom. I remember praying as a young girl that marriage and motherhood would be part of God's plan for me. And I was delighted when He answered my prayer. But then imagine my amazement when God asked me to help "birth" a worldwide ministry with 20,000 groups meeting weekly, with approximately 150,000 women involved, and with a presence in ninety-one countries—a ministry that prays for children and their schools.

Moms In Touch International (MITI) began with a small prayer in my kitchen, when I faced a crisis. The year was 1984, the place was British Columbia, Canada. My husband, Rle (pronounced Ar-lee), and I had four children. The first three were boys, and since Rle coached the Athletes in Action basketball team for Campus Crusade for Christ, we kidded each other that we could end up giving birth to our own five-man team. But God in His perfect plan gave us one more child, and this time it was a girl.

What Can I Do?!

The day of my crisis was in September, at the beginning of the school year. I had just hugged and kissed my two eldest sons as I sent them off to the public junior high school not too far from our home. As I walked back to the kitchen, fearful thoughts formed when I considered what they would be facing. I knew the school would be a battlefield for their hearts and minds. The temptations loomed in my imagination: immorality, drugs, alcohol, pornography, vulgar language, and philosophies that would undermine their faith.

"Oh, Lord," I prayed aloud, "please protect them, enable them to see clearly the difference between right and wrong, and help them to make godly decisions."

But even after calling out to the Lord, the burden for my sons remained. The urgency to protect them from evil was intense. I cried and begged the Lord that none of my children would live a moment in Satan's kingdom, that Satan would not gleefully get one speck of their lives, and that he would have no satisfaction over any of them believing his lies. With passion comes a vision, a dream, an idea. I knew united prayer was the answer.

"Dear Father," I prayed, "there must be one other mom who would take time out of her busy schedule to pray with me."

One simple prayer and one desperate heart equaled one answer from God. He laid on my heart another mom, Linda. I immediately called her and shared my fears and concerns for our children and the school. "Linda," I said, "I feel as though I'm sending them into darkness every day. We need to protect their hearts through prayer. Would you pray with me for one hour starting next week?"

Her response was a quick yes. Then we thought of other moms who would also want to pray, and the following week we had five women in my home.

I established a format for our time called "The Four Steps of Prayer": praise, confession, thanksgiving, and intercession. We started and ended on time. We prayed rather than talked about praying. And everything was held in confidence. That time became our hour of hope as we lifted our concerns and our children's needs to the Lord through united prayer. And when the answers to prayer came, we experienced the joy of rejoicing with each other.

The Birthing Process

Little did we realize that ordinary moms, releasing God's power through prayer, were about to birth a worldwide prayer movement. As author Wesley L. Duewel says, "God has a wonderful plan by which you can have worldwide influence [through prayer]. This plan is not just for a chosen few. It is for you."

I didn't know God was calling us to birth anything. But oftentimes big things grow out of obedience to small things.

We were growing in our faith, we were learning how to pray, and we were living the joy of seeing God answer our prayers; we couldn't help but enthusiastically tell our friends. And word got around quickly. We realized we needed to give our group a name; so we asked God to help us choose one. In unity we agreed on Moms In Touch: moms who are in touch with God, their children, their schools, and one another through prayer.

> *Little did we realize that ordinary moms, releasing God's power through prayer, were about to birth a world-wide prayer movement.*

Just as the ministry was beginning to blossom, the Athletes in Action team was relocated to Poway in southern California. "California!" I wailed. "Do Christians live in California?" I already missed Moms In Touch, and our family hadn't even moved yet.

As soon as we were settled in our new home, I prayed, "Lord, please bring me one other mom to pray with me for Poway High School."

A few weeks after school started, the Holy Spirit prompted me to thank God for the mom, as if I already had found her. So I prayed, "Father, thank You that today You are going to bring me another mom to pray with."

Later that afternoon a mother from up the street came to look for her son. As we stood in the driveway, the conversation opened to spiritual things, and I told Suzie about Moms In Touch.

She took my hand and said, "Fern, if it's just the two of us, we'll pray."

By the end of the school year, ten women were praying for Poway High School, and other groups had formed.

We regularly received letters from moms who had heard about our group and wanted my notes, typed on 8 1/2-by-11 sheets, on how to start one of their own. Soon groups were forming in other states. The requests grew.

How were we going to keep up with the demand and pay for the materials and postage? We passed the hat at my Moms In Touch group after the prayer time. As those women willingly gave, the expenses always were covered.

Through the help and encouragement of one of the group members, Sondra Ball, I compiled my notes and put them in a booklet. She had a home-based florist business and gave the proceeds to print the first 500 booklets. Today more than 400,000 English booklets are in print, as well as twenty-three translations, including a Braille version. What a difference one life can make. The booklet came into existence and took our message around the world because of Sondra's vision and sacrifice.

So many women like Sondra brought their little loaves and fishes those first years. And Jesus took what they gave, blessed it, and multiplied it. Five cookie-baking moms formed the first MITI board, gathered around my dining room table, desperately leaning on the Lord to administrate the fledgling ministry. Sondra Ball, Jackie Fitz, Carolyn Taylor, and Charlotte Domville sacrificially gave of themselves so that mothers around the country could learn of this life-changing way to pray. When I think back, we didn't always know the next steps, but we knew who did. We sought God's face continually. He never failed us.

Ripples on the Water

Author Roy Lessin says, "When a stone is dropped into a lake it quickly disappears from sight, but its impact leaves behind a series of ripples that broaden and reach across the water. In the same way, the impact of one life lived for Christ will leave behind an influence for good that will reach the lives of many others."

Beatriz Grigoni, a Hispanic mom in one of our groups in San Diego, created one such ripple. "Oh," she said, "my people in Mexico need to know how to pray for their children and schools." So the Lord prompted her to translate the MITI booklet into Spanish. Because of her, not only women in Mexico but also in Spain, the United States, Central America, and South America are gathering together to say prayers for their children in Spanish.

Another ripple in the water was made by Connie Kennemer. In January 1988, Connie chaired our first MITI retreat. Thirty-five moms gathered at the Pine Valley Conference Center to grow in their faith, to be trained, and to expect revival. We settled into a cozy room with a fire crackling away in the fireplace. We began by asking God that every school in San Diego County would have a MITI group. The prayers grew bolder. We asked for all of California. The Holy Spirit prompted our hearts to be bolder yet. We asked God for all the states along the West Coast; then we moved right across the United States. But then came a big stretch of faith. We asked for a MITI group for every school in the world.

One woman prayed, "But, Lord, who can tell all these moms? . . . Dr. Dobson, that's who! Lord, we ask that we could get on his radio program." I think a few women giggled.

But a couple of months later, LuAnne Crane, the assistant producer for the Focus on the Family radio broadcast, called to say she kept hearing good things about our organization and wanted to know more. As I shared with her, she caught the vision of the ministry and promised she would write it down the best she could and give it to Dr. Dobson. But, she cautioned, "hundreds of things cross his desk, and he will make the final decision about your being on the program." Boy, did we pray!

In April, twelve moms traveled with me to Focus on the Family headquarters in Pomona, California, so they could pray while I was being interviewed. Dr. Dobson invited all of us into his office to get acquainted before the program. He asked each woman, "Now, tell me, what does Moms In Touch mean to you?" Some of the women sniffled as they shared while others had tears trickling down their cheeks. We used a lot of Kleenex.

But all eyes widened and several mouths gaped when Dr. Dobson proclaimed, "Let's set up twelve more chairs; we're going to have them all on the air."

We had asked God for a two-day program just in case a mom missed the first day. Well, God gave us three. Women were hungry to hear how they could unite together to protect their children's hearts through prayer. More than 20,000 responses came as a result of the broadcast. Needless to say, the ministry has never been the same since. God answered the prayers of moms who dared to ask big.

Through the sacrifices and belief of so many women, Moms In Touch became the international movement it is today. That small prayer I uttered in my kitchen out of desperation for my children was the beginning of women drawing together around the world. For mothers' hearts everywhere—regardless of culture, political climate, or economic circumstance—are the same. Every mother feels the need to pray for her child. And every child needs a praying mom.

Part 1

Responding to the Call to Pray

1. *A Song of Prayer*

God has given each of us a song that only we can sing. The song is His special calling and purpose, an offering only one person can make to Him. No one else can hum your tune. And if it were not sung, it would be sorely missed.

Part of the song each individual is to sing is expressed through prayer. God wants to hear from each of us. And our prayer-song, even if we think it's an ordinary tune, can have great power.

Do you feel your prayers are powerful? That they affect the outcome of situations? That they cause God to bend down and incline His ear toward you? Or do you feel your notes are off-key rather than a sweet melody? Or perhaps you often remain silent because you're afraid you don't know how to pray well enough. Or maybe you feel discouraged because you've tried to pray, but the experience wasn't what you had hoped.

As we begin our exploration about prayer, I assure you that, regardless how tentative the notes of your prayer-song, God longs to hear from you. And whether you sing a solo, a duet, or in a group, He listens long and well. Your melody pleases Him, even if you think your song is too simple, too small, or too petty (those "help me find a parking space" prayers).

Prayer Changes

I've written this book to boost your confidence in prayer and in your ability to pray. I want you to believe deeply and fervently that praying is one of the most important contributions you can make to your child's life—and that that contribution will have long-term results, results that will unfold even when you're no longer on earth. To that end, together we're going to try out some new prayer-songs, consider from Scripture what God thinks about our prayers, be encouraged to keep on praying even when we have to hold our notes longer than we ever thought we could, and hear from other moms who have prayed long and hard. My prayer is that by the time you finish this book, you'll be excited, energized, and enlightened about your prayer life. But even more important, you'll be changed. For while prayer sometimes changes circumstances and can even change other people's minds, it almost always changes the heart of the pray-er.

I recall one prayer group I participated in, in which we prayed with a mom who was distraught over her relationship with her son. He hated her so much he would wince at her touch. The wall between them was high and wide. We prayed week after week for the relationship to heal. We asked God to tear down the wall of bitterness, resentment, and anger. We prayed that the mom would see things she might be doing that kept her son on the other side of that wall.

By the end of the school year, the son was hugging his mom before he left for school. Who changed? I'm sure the mom would say that God changed her and that enabled her son to change, but truthfully, God changed them both.

Not that praying isn't hard work. It is. But God's answers often amaze us. That's part of what makes praying so exciting. Many times in our prayer group we experienced immediate answers to prayer, but with some prayers we didn't see anything happen. A foster son was on drugs and alcohol. We prayed fervently for this handsome young man. Yet we saw no change. Actually, things grew worse. We persevered, praying that he would love God and serve Him with a devoted heart. Throughout his junior and senior high years and into his adult life, he continued on the road to self-destruction. But God heard the prayers of us moms, crying out for his life, and He answered—twenty years later. I just received a letter from his foster mom joyously sharing how this son surrendered his life to Christ, married a Christian girl, and is actively involved in a local church. As his coworkers watched the transformation in his life, they asked him lots of questions about the changes. But what is really above and beyond what we could have imagined, as we prayed in our small group all those years before, was that he would lead his birth mother to the Lord before she died.

The Song Sung over Me

Now, I don't want you to think that my prayer-song bubbled up as a surprise one day and I prayed fervently and well from then on. I'm learning about prayer every day, just like you. But I did see prayer's power in the life of someone close to me—my mom. She prayed throughout the day in our home, always leading us in prayer before meals and at bedtime. Many times she would pray in the car before we left the driveway to ask for God's protection. And on Wednesday nights, Mom would take us to church for the weekly prayer meeting. I can remember sitting in a church pew when I was still so young that my legs dangled midair, unable to reach the floor. I listened as the saints' prayers filled the room. I never grew impatient or bored. Quite the contrary, I never felt more at home than when I was in the safe, secure love of those prayers. Whether at home, coming and going in the car, or at church, my mother demonstrated that a loving God cared about me and was attentive to hear and answer my prayers. As a result, I asked Jesus into my heart as a young girl. I can't remember a time in my life that I haven't talked to my heavenly Father.

The Difference One Prayer Can Make

I've seen such wonderful answers to prayer over the years—including in my own family—that those answers spur me on to keep praying. While we lived in British Columbia, my husband, Rle, and our ten-year-old son, Troy, were invited to go on a canoe trip with a friend and his son. The friend had canoed down the Fraser River many times, and he wanted to share the fun with Rle. Besides, it would be a great adventure for the two boys.

Excitement built as the day grew closer. Much preparation and planning preceded the event.

Because it was early spring, the snowcap was melting off the mountains, causing the river to run high and rapid. The day of the trip turned out wet and rainy, but that didn't deter these hearty souls.

After packing the canoe with their supplies, they were about to launch the boat when they heard voices calling out to them. Two men who were coming ashore were yelling.

"You aren't going out on the river, are you?" one of the men shouted.

When the man who had invited my husband said, "Yes," one of the strangers responded, "I wouldn't go out today. The water's too high and swift. We'll be picking you up off the bottom."

Rle's friend assured my husband that he had canoed the river in all kinds of weather and they would be fine. Still, as they jumped into the canoe, Rle saw the two strangers shaking their heads in disbelief.

About mid-afternoon I felt prompted to pray for Rle and Troy's protection. So strong was the impression that I stopped what I was doing, sat down at the kitchen table with my Bible, and claimed promises of protection for them. I prayed: "Protect them from the evil one" (John 17:15). "Those who trust in the LORD are like Mount Zion, which cannot be shaken but endures forever. As the mountains surround Jerusalem, so the LORD surrounds his people both now and forevermore" (Psalm 125:1–2). "'Because he loves me,' says the LORD, 'I will rescue him; I will protect him, for he acknowledges my name'" (Psalm 91:14).

Then I prayed for Rle's friend and his son, "Lord, You know what is happening right now. I ask that You would protect them. Keep them safe. Put Your arms around them and keep them close to You. Bring them home. I trust You; I will not be shaken. Oh, Lord, bring them home." I must have prayed for almost an hour.

God Answers

Later that evening I received a call from my worn-out yet thankful husband. As he told me what had happened that afternoon, I calculated the time and realized the terrifying story had taken place just when the Holy Spirit had prompted me to pray.

Rle's story unfolded like this: As they paddled down the river, they picked up speed until suddenly they hit a drop-off, like a small waterfall. The canoe shot into the air, and all its occupants were thrown into the icy river. As Rle came to his senses, he realized he was underwater, held there by two little feet on top of his shoulders. Not knowing where the strength came from, he hoisted Troy off of him and swam with Troy to the canoe, which was nearby and hadn't sunk. He pulled up Troy to get his chest out of the water because Rle was concerned about hypothermia.

Troy asked him, "Daddy, are we going to die?"

Rle was silently resolute.

Troy continued, "It's okay, Daddy. We'll be with Jesus."

The friend and his son were farther away from the canoe. Rle said he would never forget the sound of his friend frantically calling for his son and the relief when father and son found each other in the roiling water. God gave them the strength to swim toward the canoe and latch on.

After forty-five minutes of battling the freezing, raging waters, their strength was giving way and they were chilled to the bone. Just as Rle was comprehending that they really were going to die, another miracle occurred.

They felt land under their feet and discovered a small, submerged island in the middle of the river. They were barely able to stand because of the water rushing over the island. Shaking uncontrollably they huddled together in prayer, thanking Jesus for their momentary safety.

Then, in a matter of minutes a helicopter, with just enough space to land, picked them up and whisked them to a nearby hospital. How had the rescue crew known? Another miracle. A couple saw the accident and immediately called for help. The paramedics said that if Troy had been in the water ten more minutes he would have died of hypothermia.

What a privilege I had to fight for the physical lives of my loved ones and their friends through prayer. Did my prayer make a difference? Did God send ministering angels to help because I prayed? Yes and yes. God promises that when I call to Him, He hears me and will do great and mighty things. Prayer can make the difference between life and death.

Singing Your Song

Why pray? Because the power of one praying life is of great value. Don't quit. Your prayers can only be sung by you.

"Actions in heaven begin when someone prays on earth," said pastor and author Max Lucado. "You may not understand the mystery of your task. But this much is clear: When you speak, Jesus hears."

> **Did my prayer make a difference? Did God send ministering angels to help because I prayed? Yes and yes.**

I can't help but think of the verse in James, "The earnest (heartfelt, continued) prayer of a righteous man makes tremendous power available—dynamic in its working" (James 5:16, AMP).

Family members pulled to safety, children released from drug abuse, and family relationships restored—these are only a sampling of the great effect a life of prayer can have.

In upcoming chapters we'll explore how to pray four life-changing prayers; overcome our own barriers that hold us back from praying powerfully; pray for our loved ones using Scripture; pray according to God's will; claim God's promises in prayer; fight spiritual battles on behalf of our children in prayer; and pray no matter what.

In the next chapter we'll examine one of the biggest barriers to prayer—struggling to believe that God truly hears and responds to our prayers. How can you become a confident pray-er, even when God doesn't answer?

And now, I'd like to close this chapter in prayer for you. In upcoming chapters, I'll provide a prayer for you to offer as a song at the end of each chapter. But for now, let me pray this prayer over you:

> *Sovereign Lord, thank You for how much You love and value every single person. Each life has a song given by You that only that person can sing. I pray that not one*

of Your children would doubt the power of her song. Give her the courage to trust You. May Your love cast out fear so that she can sing the song You have given with confidence. Oh, Father, may she bring You great honor and glory as You are faithful to help her sing her song. In Jesus' name, amen.

2. Becoming a Confident Pray-er

I'm inspired by the story of William Carey's sister. William was a missionary who labored in India for forty-two years in the mid to late 1800s. He and his coworkers translated the Bible into twenty-five Indian languages. Many books have been written about him, and rightly so.

But William Carey's sister seems not to have received mention until Warren and Ruth Myers wrote *Pray*, in which they tell her amazing story. Mary, William's youngest sister, whom he called "Polly," was bedridden and almost completely paralyzed for fifty-two years. But she was close to God and to her brother.

William wrote to her the details of his struggles in creating Indian grammar books, primers, and dictionaries. He described the difficulties of figuring out how to get books typed and Bibles printed. As he sent these details to her in London, she lifted them to the Lord in prayer, faithfully offering up many hours of prayer "work," asking God to meet her brother's needs year after year. As Warren and Ruth Myers say, "To whose account will God credit the victories won through this remarkable man?"[1]

What a woman of faith Polly was to never let her physical disability paralyze her prayer life. What was her secret that enabled her to pray with such fervor and consistency over so many years? Where did she find her confidence?

Barrier to Praying

Like Polly, we all experience barriers to praying, but perhaps one of the biggest is our lack of confidence. You might not be confident in your ability to say the right words. Or maybe you aren't sure God is even listening. Or possibly you figure God is listening, but He isn't in the mood to answer.

Kellie, for example, was fearful of praying in a group. "I felt unqualified to pray from my heart because I grew up praying only by rote. 'Who am I to pray so boldly?' I asked myself. 'I'm not in ministry or a trained layperson.'"

Plus Kellie was concerned that her prayers wouldn't sound as eloquent as everyone else's. And she was embarrassed that her son, who at one point had given his life to God, was depressed, drank excessively, and was rebelling against the Lord. How could someone with such a child pray with others whose lives were much more . . . well, spiritual?

Desperate about her son, who continued to sink deeper into rebellion and depression, she decided she needed to join a Moms In Touch prayer group. Now, if she could just find the courage to go to a meeting and pray . . .

Then one day, as Kellie answered the phones at the Poway, California, health facility where she worked, a caller responded to Kellie's greeting by saying, "This is Fern Nichols."

"My heart pounded when I heard that," Kellie recalls. "I knew God was pulling and dragging me to MITI." Yet fear still overwhelmed her. She swallowed hard and then said, "I know you're the president of Moms In Touch."

She tells me I responded with, "Oh, do you have children?"

Kellie later told me she felt divided about whether she should confess that she had a child who was in trouble. So she answered, "Yes, our freshman daughter is a strong Christian, and our troubled son is out of school." She figured since he wasn't in school, this answer would get her off the hook and she wouldn't have to be involved in MITI.

"We have a college and career group," came my response. "Would you like to ride with me on Thursday?"

Kellie figured God had her cornered. She really was going to have to go to the group now. So we went together, and when the group divided into twos for prayer, we were paired. Later Kellie admitted she felt uneasy praying with me because she saw me as the founder of an international prayer ministry.

But Kellie said she felt peace and knew she was in the right place at the right time to do the right thing—to pray about her son with someone who had a mother's heart just like hers. That was how Kellie began to gain confidence in her ability to pray and in God's eagerness to listen. Eventually, after almost dying from a ruptured appendix, her son had a spiritual turnaround and realized that prayer had brought him through his life-threatening situation.

The Source for Confidence

How did Polly Carey and Kellie find the confidence to believe that God would hear and answer their prayers? As simple as this might seem, they knew they were God's children. God is, in a sense, like a mom who recognizes her child's voice amid a whole chorus of children, all of whom might be calling out "Mom" at the same time. A mother responds to her child because she knows the sound of his or her voice. So, too, God responds to our call because He knows the sound of our voice.

Consider Barbara Lea, who wanted more than anything to feel like a child of God. But because of her lifestyle, she doubted He could ever love her or forgive her—let alone answer her prayers.

Barbara Lea started to drink in the eleventh grade and added marijuana and partying during college. Then came a coat hanger abortion, two failed marriages (one of her husbands was abusive), and sleeping around with a number of men. The drug abuse escalated with her taking speed during the day to get through work and then a joint at night to help her relax. Snorting cocaine was a regular part of her life too.

As time went by, Barbara Lea and her divorced boss, with whom she shared a small office, found solace with each other. Eventually Barbara Lea realized she had fallen in love with Howard.

"Then he asked me if I would be committed to him," Barbara Lea said. "For the first time in my life, I had a man who loved me, and all he asked me for was a commitment. A commitment? What was that? The only thing I had been committed to in my thirty-four years was maybe a job.... I don't recall ever even thinking of that word before. After I munched on that thought for a while, I decided that, yes, I could do that.

"A friend suggested Howard and I attend her church. I immediately knew I had been missing something important that this church fulfilled for me. Even Howard liked attending it.

"You have to realize what state I was in—still doing drugs and living with Howard as an unmarried woman. But at one particular Sunday evening service, I remember marveling how awesome God was to His people. Firm but gentle, kind, compassionate, loving unconditionally, and committed.... *There's that word again ... God wants me to be committed to Him too. Can I do that? But what about all I've done ... what I'm still doing? Ah, He is also forgiving ... could He forgive me too?*

"As if hearing my internal question, the pastor then said, 'John 3:16 tells us, "For God so loved the world that he gave his one and only Son, that whoever believes in him shall not perish but have eternal life."' He went on to say, 'Tonight some of you might not have fully trusted your lives to God, or maybe your path has taken a wrong turn.'

"*Is the pastor looking at me?*

"The pastor continued, 'John 14:6 says, "Jesus answered, 'I am the way and the truth and the life. No one comes to the Father except through me.'"' Jesus has a gift for you. Ephesians 2:8–9 reminds us, "For it is by grace you have been saved, through faith—and this not from yourselves, it is a gift of God—not by works, so that no one can boast." I would like to give you an opportunity now to receive Christ as your personal Lord and Savior, to accept His forgiveness and His unconditional love for you.'

"*But I've been the giver in all my relationships. You mean God wants to give me this amazing gift? How do I receive?*

"'Please bow your heads and close your eyes,' the pastor directed. 'If you feel Him speaking to you right now, repeat this prayer after me silently in your heart.'

"My heart was pounding. I wanted to pray that prayer, to become a child of God.

"The prayer was something like, 'Lord Jesus, I need You. Thank You for dying on the cross for my sins. I want to receive You as my Lord and Savior. Thank You for forgiving my sins and giving me eternal life. I want You to take control of my life, Jesus. Make me the person You want me to be.'

"A joy rushed through me that I can't possibly explain. It was almost like the hard crust around my heart was falling off.

"On the way out of the service, Howard and I each told the other that we had accepted Christ.

"I struggled for a few months because I was hooked on speed. The drying out period was the pits, but I know it could have been much worse after twenty years of drug abuse. But I did end my drugs, drinking, and partying, and Howard and I got married. We've been together ever since. Our blended family has caused us real difficulties, but we've worked hard to repair the damage we caused to so many before we accepted Christ. But now I know I'm forgiven, I'm a child of God, and He's eager to hear my prayers."

Joining the Family

Your life might not involve the excesses that Barbara Lea's did, but we all have behaved in ways that need forgiving. Have you invited Christ into your life? Do you have doubts about your salvation? If so, may I encourage you to make this most important decision of your life? You can become a child of God. There truly is no greater decision than accepting Jesus Christ as your Lord and Savior. If your heart has been touched and you sense your heavenly Father wooing you to Himself, you could pray a prayer like Barbara Lea did. "Thank You for dying on the cross for my sins and for giving me eternal life. I want to receive You as my Lord and Savior. Jesus, make me the person You want me to be. Amen." The precise words aren't what matter. God responds to the sincerity of your heart, not the eloquence of your words. Take this moment to make that decision now ... If you have just received Christ as your Lord and Savior, I want to welcome you to God's family; you're now God's child.

God's heart toward each of us, His children, is expressed in these verses. Contemplate, meditate on, and ponder these amazing truths.

> You are loved forever (Jeremiah 31:3).
> You are His own possession, His special treasure (Exodus 19:5).
> You were created in His own image (Genesis 1:27).
> You are the one in whom He delights (Isaiah 42:1).
> You are precious and honored in His sight (Isaiah 43:4).
> You are the apple of His eye (Deuteronomy 32:10).
> You are His glorious inheritance (Ephesians 1:18).

Have you ever felt so loved, so special, and so accepted? "How great is the love the Father has lavished on us, that we should be called children of God!" (1 John 3:1).

My daughter-in-law, whom I call my daughter-in-love, Bonnie, had our grandson fingerprinted to make sure that, if he ever got lost, he would be identified and returned home. His fingerprints are a sure way of knowing who he is and to whom he belongs. When we accept Christ, we belong to God. We can never get lost because we are partakers of the divine nature (1 Peter 1:4). "Therefore, if anyone is in Christ, he is a new creation [new person]; the old has gone, the new has come!" (2 Corinthians 5:17). Your identity has changed, you have become someone new, you have new "fingerprints."

Immediate Access

As God's children, we have the right, the privilege, the identity, the "fingerprint" to talk to God anytime, anywhere, anyplace. We don't have to be announced, placed on a list, or wait our turn. As His children, we have immediate access.

We're like the little boy John F. Kennedy Jr., who blitzed right into his daddy's Oval Office, climbed up on his daddy's lap, and received his daddy's full attention. He was oblivious that his father was the president or that he might have interrupted an important meeting. He just wanted to be with his dad so he went in—unannounced—yet received.

> As God's children, we have the right, the privilege, the identity, the "fingerprint" to talk to God anytime, anywhere, anyplace. We don't have to be announced, placed on a list, or wait our turn.

As God's children, we have immediate access to the King of Kings, our Dad, but it wasn't always that way. In the Old Testament only the high priests could go into the inner place, the Most Holy Place, to pray for their sins and the people's sins. But because of Jesus' death and resurrection, He opened the way for us to enter as well.

I love how the book of Hebrews explains it:

> But only the high priest went into the inner room, and then only once a year, all alone, and always with blood which he sprinkled on the mercy seat as an offering to God to cover his own mistakes and sins, and the mistakes and sins of all the people. And the Holy Spirit uses all this to point out to us that under the old system the common people could not go into the Holy of Holies. . . . He [Jesus] came as High Priest of this better system which we now have. He went into that greater, perfect tabernacle in heaven, not made by men nor part of this world, and once for all took blood into that inner room, the Holy of Holies, and sprinkled it on the mercy seat; . . . he took his own blood, and with it he, by himself, made sure of our eternal salvation. *And so, dear brothers, now we may walk right into the very Holy of Holies where God is, because of the blood of Jesus.* (Hebrews 9:7–8, 11–12; 10:19, TLB, italics mine)

Did you let that truth grab your heart? Do you know what it means? Once you understand this concept, it will change the way you pray. We are not only children of God but also priests. We not only have the privilege of coming to God's throne, but we can also bring prayers for others with us, just as the priests in the Old Testament did. They didn't go only for themselves; they took prayers for the whole nation with them.

Pastor Ron Dunn elaborates, "The Bible says, you are a kingdom of priests. That doesn't mean just that you have the right to go into the presence of God, but it also means you have the right and the obligation to take others with you into that presence."

Remember the canoe story in the first chapter? When I prayed for the safety of my husband, my son, and their two friends, I was taking hold of my identity as a child of God and as a priest to come with confidence to my Father. I had immediate access to the Creator of heaven and earth, my "Dad."

Confidence Despite God's Silence

Knowing who you are in Christ gives you confidence in those times when you have prayed and prayed but haven't seen the answer to your prayer. I remember one time when I had prayed for my son for months. He wasn't walking with the Lord. On one particular day, as I was praying, I was feeling worn and weak in my faith. Was God really hearing my prayer? Was I asking with enough faith?

I asked the Lord to remind me of who I was in Christ, and I began to rehearse the truths of the authority given to me as His daughter and priest. This is the prayer that poured from my heart, "Father, I bring to You my son. He is not following You. He is going his own way. He is making decisions that are hurting his testimony and his walk with You. Thank You for reminding me of Your command to rebuke Satan and to tell him to flee. On the authority of who I am in Christ and what You have told me to do, I will do it in the name of Jesus.

"Satan and demon powers, in the mighty name of Lord Jesus, I command you to let go of my son. You cannot have him. He belongs to Jesus. Now flee.

"Father, thank You that Jesus, who is in me, is greater than Satan, who is in the world. I hold up Your word of promise for my son, that You have begun a good work in his life and You will continue that good work until Jesus comes. You are not a God who lies or a man who changes his mind. What You have promised You will fulfill. In Jesus' name, amen."

I continued to resist Satan in the name of Jesus and laid hold of God's promises. What a privilege as a mom to take up my priestly position and to come boldly before God's throne, interceding with confidence for mercy and help for my son.

I realized that day that if I don't believe who I am in Christ and don't exercise the rights I have as a priest in His kingdom, it's as if I didn't have the inheritance of a child or the authority of a priest. By the way, God answered my prayer. My son is walking with the Lord and serving Him on his church's worship team.

Taking Loved Ones to the Holy Place

How often are you coming into God's presence? The privilege, the power, the authority is yours. Do you think that Satan could be running rampant in your home because you're not bringing your husband into the Holy of Holies as often as you should? God wants to work in your husband's life, as He wants to work in yours. But God wants you to take him into the holy place. Are you taking your children in, claiming the Word of God for them? Are you taking your mother-in-law in ... your mother ... your neighbor ... your unsaved friends?

Are you so faithful that God can lay a burden on your heart to pray for something specific and know that you will?

I want to share with you a story that shows the importance of faithful pray-ers. In 1986 the mission chairman of Park Street Church in Boston confirmed all the details were true. Park Street Church supports a medical missionary named Dr. Bob Foster in Angola. The Marxist forces had control of Angola; however, guerrilla resistance to the new regime continued in the area around the medical clinic Dr. Foster ran.

One day Dr. Foster sent a coworker on an errand to a city some miles away with the warning that he should be back by nightfall. The stretch of road between the clinic and the city went through the jungle area where most of the guerrilla fighting took place, and it was dangerous to travel through there at night. Well, the coworker went on his way, finished his errands in plenty of time, and began his return.

Much to his dismay, however, his van developed engine trouble and broke down in the middle of the jungle. With no other cars on the road, he had no choice but to lock the doors, pray, and attempt to get a little rest.

Amazingly, he slept through till morning without a problem. He caught a ride into town for some spare parts, fixed the van, and completed the trip back to the clinic.

A relieved Dr. Foster and other coworkers greeted him. "Oh, we are so thankful to see you," Dr. Foster told him. "We heard sounds of heavy fighting last night." Dr. Foster's assistant said he had heard nothing and had seen nothing.

Shortly after that a guerrilla leader came to the clinic to be treated, and Dr. Foster asked him if he had seen a van stalled along the highway the previous night.

"Yes," replied the man.

"Well, why didn't you take possession of it?" asked the doctor.

"We started to until we got closer, and then we saw that it was heavily guarded. Twenty-seven well-armed government soldiers surrounded it."

The incident remained a mystery until Dr. Foster's assistant returned to the States on furlough. Person after person on his prayer team came up to him, twenty-seven people in all, to say that the Lord had given them a special burden to pray for him the day he had been stranded in the jungle.[2]

What if only two would have been found faithful to pray when the Holy Spirit prompted them? Perhaps the guerrillas would have taken possession of the van because only two guarded it. But God counted on twenty-seven to pray, and the prayers of those high priests on the missionary's prayer team kept him safe.

God allowed His Son's precious blood to be spilled so as His child I could come to Him any time. My audience with God doesn't need to be put on His calendar, and I won't be kept waiting. I can cry out to Him on behalf of myself, and I can bring a whole nation, a missionary, or my family with me. And I can come with confidence.

Let this verse encourage your heart and remind you that you too have the rights and privileges of a child of God and of a priest to pray with confidence—not hesitancy, fear, or uncertainty—but with confidence. "This is the confidence we have in approaching God: that if we ask anything according to his will, he hears us. And if we know that he hears us—whatever we ask—we know that we have what we asked of him" (1 John 5:14–15).

> *Dear God, thank You that I am Your child. And because of that You experience pleasure and delight in me—how amazing that is. I don't need to be meek or timid or shy when I come into Your presence. And thank You that I also have the responsibility and privilege of being a priest who, because of Jesus' blood, can pray not only for myself but also for others. Help me to bear that responsibility with diligence and honor. I want to come boldly to Your throne and to receive Your mercy and to find grace in time of need (Hebrews 4:16 TLB).*

3. Life-Changing Prayer

Many times when our children were growing up, we would try to have cozy dinners like we had seen in Norman Rockwell's paintings. I would prepare the menu, hunt up recipes, grocery shop, and make each dish with love and care. As I diced, sliced, stirred, and mixed, I envisioned the dinnertime conversation and pictured an atmosphere of calm, quiet, and unhurriedness.

But sometimes when dinner was served, the Norman Rockwell scene morphed into a busy, contemporary piece of art that dazzled the eyes and confused the senses. Especially during our children's teenage years, drama practices, sporting events, and social lives pushed them out the door so fast I felt as if I were left with my fork suspended over my barely started supper. "Thanks, Mom, for the meal," they would call out. "It was great but gotta go now. See you later." Bear any resemblance to some dinners at your house?

Ah, but on the holidays, at our house, time always is set aside for family, celebration, and food. What wonderful laughter, conversation, and entertaining stories are served up at dinnertime. My favorite moment is when dessert is unveiled. It seems the longer we sup together, the more relaxed everyone becomes. The conversation flows freely, and stories are told that probably wouldn't have been shared otherwise. Lingering around the table is delicious.

That's what our heavenly Father loves too, that uninterrupted time of lingering over dessert. Having free, open communication. But so often we rush in to have a quick bite and call out, "Catch ya later,

God," as we hurry onto the next item on our to-do list. Many times we don't stay long enough to have dinner at all.

Do you struggle to sit still long enough to hear God's quiet voice? To think about what you want to tell Him? To quiet the frenzied listing of shoulds and musts that consumes much of your day?

In this chapter, we'll examine four life-changing types of prayers that will revitalize your time with God and make you eager to "sit and sup" with Him. But before we launch into specific ways to talk with our Father, let's take a look at what keeps us from praying and why we must overcome those hindrances.

Twirling Plates

Remember the circus act in which a man whirls plates on top of tall poles? He begins by placing a plate on top of the first pole. He spins the pole, making the plate swirl to a momentum that keeps the plate from falling off. Then he moves to the second pole, sets the plate to swirling, and moves on down the line of poles. When he reaches the sixth pole, the first pole begins to wobble. The crowd shouts, causing the performer to run to the first pole, just in the nick of time to save the plate. Is that a picture of your life? So busy that you're frantically running here and there, trying to juggle all the plates, constantly sacrificing the first plate, which is your quiet time in prayer with the Father? You can become so frazzled you don't have time for God to reveal Himself and His love. You miss out on His sustenance that enables you, whatever difficulties you encounter that day, confidently to handle them through Him. You forfeit the light He can shed on those things that confuse you. And you see no answered prayer.

Yet, if you think about it, you manage to find time to spend with the people you love. I know I can hardly wait to baby-sit my grandson every Friday night. I anticipate singing to him and pushing his stroller up and down the street with grandma pride.

Maybe you and I lack that same enthusiasm for being with Jesus. I know sometimes I struggle to remember the benefits of spending time with Him. Often I've prayed my own version of Paul's impassioned longing in Philippians 3:10: "Loving Lord, I want to know You and the power of Your resurrection. I want to feel Your touch. I want to love You with a deeper, more intimate love. Make me passionate for You."

I like knowing that Jesus' table always is set; He's just waiting for me to join Him. Author Warren Myers says, "Our Father, who thinks of us constantly, eagerly awaits our every visit home, whether we come for a few minutes, a half hour, or an afternoon."[1] Realizing God is waiting helps me to set aside the time to talk, just as I would for a friend who had prepared a lovely tea for me.

Part of the reason it's hard to set that time aside is that Satan tries everything in his power to keep you from it. He wants you to think that being spiritual means being productive. He doesn't want you to cross over the invisible line into powerful, life-changing prayer. If he can keep you thinking that being on the productive side of the line is doing great things for God, then you will secure few blessings for yourself, your family, your children's schools, your community, and your country. But if you cross over the line to commune with God, He will move heaven and earth to answer your prayers, and you will see great victories and Satan's defeat. Satan knows he has no power against your prayers.

Plan to Neglect

I've found that if I'm to keep my zeal and passion for God, I must "plan to neglect" anything that would hinder me from prayer. Like anything that brings about great results, prayer requires discipline. It's a matter of the will. Every day I have to decide if I'm going to spend time with the Father. It's not a once-and-for-all decision.

> *I've found that if I'm to keep my zeal and passion for God, I must "plan to neglect" anything that would hinder me from prayer.*

This morning, despite plenty of plates to juggle on their poles, I chose to pray. And in my prayers was a request for my family's safety. How thankful I am I took that time because, just as I was writing this chapter, I was interrupted by a phone call from my daughter, Trisha.

"Mom, I was in an accident," she said as soon as I answered the phone. She had stopped her car for a red light and a young driver had run into her vehicle. After I found out that she and the other driver were okay and I assured her that the insurance information she had obtained was what was needed, we hung up. Then it occurred to me how thankful I was that I hadn't let the busyness of life gobble up my time that morning, but that I had asked God to protect each family member.

As we face the choice of how to distribute our time each day, this poem helps to put the options into perspective.

The Wrong Race

Lord, it's been such a busy day,
and I never even stopped to pray.
Now the day is almost through,
and I'm just too tired to talk to you.

This pace of life is so very busy,
the thought of tomorrow makes me dizzy.
I'm already worried about the weather,
and all the plans I must pull together.

Lord, will this craziness ever stop,
or must I always strive to stay on top?
I look forward to the day when I see Jesus face to face,
when He opens His arms to give me an embrace.

But as He looks deep into my weary eyes,
His words may come as quite a surprise.
"You have lived your life at a ridiculous pace,
and I'm sorry to say you chose the wrong race.

You hurried and hustled each and every day,
but all I wanted was to hear you pray.
I would have taken you under my wing,
and given you strength to do the important things."

The moral of the story is easy to see,
Jesus doesn't want what's left, He first wants me.

Diane Elliot

I know many women would agree that praying each day is important. But then they confess, "I don't know where to begin. What do I actually do in a quiet time?"

The "Four Steps of Prayer" have provided a wonderful format for me during my prayer time. The steps are praise, confession, thanksgiving, and intercession. I have learned much about prayer using this outline—and I continue to learn as I use the steps.

In this chapter I'll introduce you to each step. In upcoming chapters, we'll look at each aspect of prayer in greater depth.

1. Praising God

Start out your prayer time with praise, focusing on one of God's attributes, something that is true about Him. You become better acquainted with God through praising Him, and you begin to view your circumstances through the lens of God's character.

Ruth certainly found that true for her. "My initial response to my diagnosis of breast cancer was deeply affected by the idea of focusing on praise. My surgeon phoned me at two in the afternoon with the news. I had until three to adjust before picking up my two teens from high school. My eyes filled with tears as I paced from one room to another, talking to God. Immediately, all God's characteristics and attributes that we joyfully offer to Him in our prayer group flooded into my mind, assuring me that God was much bigger than my illness." As she rehearsed who her God was, Ruth was able to pull herself together before the three o'clock deadline. Her sons were greeted by a calm mom who was confident her God was in control.

As you learn to praise God for His attributes, you will trust Him more and more. After all, you trust a person you know. And when you praise God, you will experience, as Ruth did, a wonderful awareness of His presence.

2. Confessing to God

Following your time of praise comes a time of confession. This is a heart-searching time, asking the Holy Spirit to reveal to you any area of your life that might not be pleasing to Him. This prayer requires that you be honest with God. If we knowingly hold on to sin (behavior or thoughts that are not pleasing to God), we block our communication and fellowship with God.

Susi became aware of some specific sins during a retreat at which I spoke. She relates her story this way: "Your talk Saturday morning helped me to see the unforgiving spirit I had toward my husband. I've had troubles all our married life accepting his humanness. Instead, I've concentrated on his feebleness and foibles. I've listened to Satan's lies and believed if I were a better wife, my husband would be a more godly man. All this did was make me more dissatisfied with my husband and with me. After the session I had barely closed the door to my room when I cried and confessed that sin to God. The burden of all the other stuff in our marriage immediately was lifted because of my confession of anger with my husband. I'm eager to go home and ask his forgiveness for my attitude and unreal expectations."

Jesus never intended for us to carry around sin; He forgave all our sin at the cross. Susi humbled herself, told God she was sorry, and made it right with her husband. The murky, clogged communication with her heavenly Father was cleansed by Jesus' forgiving blood.

3. Giving Thanks to God

The third step is to offer prayers of thanksgiving, expressing appreciation and gratefulness for God's answers. During this segment of your prayer time, don't ask for anything, only offer thanks. The apostle Paul tells us that we are to give thanks in all things (1 Thessalonians 5:18). When this command is obeyed, it produces a grateful heart, which pleases the Lord (Psalm 50:23).

Even if the answer to your prayers is contrary to what you asked, your thanksgiving expresses confidence in God's plan, crowding out fear and discouragement. A heart that is thankful is humble and trusting. The benefit of giving thanks is priceless—God's rest! Habitually giving thanks also will produce a gracious spirit when a tough moment pops up and catches you by surprise.

I remember one such time when we lived in British Columbia. We had just bought a new home (an incredible miracle, as far as we were concerned). The day the house was finished, our family piled into the car and drove to the new house, feeling a mixture of glee and excitement. Never had we lived in a home without dents, dirt, leaks ... This place had not a flaw anywhere; it was perfect. We hurriedly walked up to the front door. Trisha, who was three at the time, reached the door first and flung it open. The doorknob crashed into the wall, cracking the plaster and creating a big dent. The workers had forgotten to put the rubber stopper on the baseboard to prevent such an incident. Trisha's eyes were as big as the doorknob, and her face as white as the door.

As I looked at the damaged wall, I had a choice. Through God's grace I gave thanks.

Then I was able to bend down, give Trisha a hug, and tell her I knew she didn't mean to do it. Until we could have it fixed, it would remind us all of her enthusiasm for our new home.

That might sound like a small thing to give thanks for, but I've found it's the little things that can cause irritations, grumpiness, and being out of sorts. God continues to test me in the little things, asking me, "Will you give thanks?"

4. Interceding Before the Father

The fourth step after praise, confession, and thanks is a powerful time of coming before the Father with intercessions. Simply stated, an intercessor asks God to help someone in need. An intercessor is willing to "stand in the gap" before the throne of grace for a particular need or person until the answer comes.

Praying Scripture with a person's name inserted into the verse is a powerful way to intercede. Because you're using God's own words, you're praying God's will. This practice brings certainty and hope to your heart, increasing your faith as you trust God's promise that His Word will not come back empty but will achieve its purpose (Isaiah 55:10–11).

This truth was tested in my life as I fervently prayed for my eldest son, Ty, concerning a marriage partner. I would place his name right in the verse found in 2 Corinthians 6:14, praying that Ty would "not be yoked together with unbelievers. For what do righteousness and wickedness have in common? Or what fellowship can light have with darkness?"

In high school, girls loved Ty, and Ty loved girls. He would bring home a little sweetie, cute as she could be, who didn't love Jesus. So I would love her, pray for her salvation, invite her to dinner, and then "pray her out"! I told God, "Lord, You are omniscient, knowing if she is going to accept You as Lord and Savior of her life. If she isn't, I pray You would remove her." I don't know how many girls came through our front door, but I kept praying.

During his sophomore year in college, Ty was leading worship at the small church we attended. One Sunday morning I noticed a beautiful young lady dressed in an outfit that reminded me of Anne of Green Gables come through the door. Her green skirt was full, and the matching cropped jacket spelled sweetness and modesty. I just kept my eye on her. I later learned that she was born in Kentucky and was in San Diego for Student Venture training, a ministry of Campus Crusade for Christ.

The next Sunday she wore the cutest little hat and had such an innocent air about her that in my spirit I said, "Lord, I think I could handle her in our family." Nine months later we had a garden wedding for Ty and Patti.

I have prayed 2 Corinthians 6:14 for all my children, that they would not be unequally yoked. God in His grace and goodness brought to our family two more "daughters-in-love," Bonnie and Tara, who also love the Lord with all their hearts, souls, and minds.

At that point, I continued to pray for our daughter. "Lord, You promised that You don't show favorites. I have one more to go—our precious Trisha. Bring to our Trisha a godly young man who loves You with all his heart and will love Trisha as Christ loves the Church." Once again I saw God's faithfulness, when Trisha became engaged to Chris, a man who loves the Lord—and her.

I'll discuss more about using Scripture in our prayers later, but the example of how I prayed for my children's mates illustrates how you can start in the adventure of intercessory prayer.

Let's Pray

By establishing a consistent time of reading the Word and praying, the roots of your life will grow deep into the soil of God's love. Will you decide right now to be disciplined in this most important decision? If so, pray, "Father, give me a hunger to know You. Help me to be committed to having a quiet time with You each day. In Jesus' name, amen."

How to Start:
A. Establish a Time.

Set aside time; give Him the best part of your day. As much as you can, let nothing interfere. And be determined to be unhurried.

Action point:

I will set aside _____(amount of time—10 minutes, half an hour) at _____ (6 A.M., 9 P.M.).

B. Choose a Place.

Set aside a place where you can meet God alone. Avoid distractions. (You might let the recorder take your phone messages during this time.) Prepare your place with Bible, pen, note-paper, or journal.

Action point:

My quiet place is located _____.

As you begin, expect to hear His voice. Start by praying, "Open my eyes that I may see wonderful things in your law" (Psalm 119:18).

C. Make a Plan.

Use the four steps of prayer.

> Praise—A time to praise God for who He is.
>
> Confession—A time to have a heart check.
>
> Thanksgiving—A time to thank God for what He has done.
>
> Intercession—A time to stand in the gap for people and circumstances.

God's Response

As you pray your way through the four life-changing steps, you might want to keep in mind this picture of how important our prayers are to the Creator of the universe. (I've adapted this thought from Rev. Ron Cline's message given at a missions conference.)

Angels numbering thousands upon thousands and ten thousand times ten thousand encircle God's throne. Loudly they sing, "Worthy is the Lamb, who was slain, to receive power and wealth and wisdom and strength and honor and glory and praise!" (Revelation 5:12).

Then every creature in heaven, on earth, under the earth, and in the sea sings, "To him who sits on the throne and to the Lamb be praise and honor and glory and power, for ever and ever!" (Revelation 5:13).

Suddenly Jesus stops everything. "Shh, listen . . . Someone is praying. I hear My daughter calling to Me."

It's hard to grasp that our prayers could really be so important to God that He would silence the heavenly host as they praise Him, isn't it? Revelation 5:8 says our prayers are saved in golden vials (bowls or vases). Just think, each of our prayers is a sweet incense to the Lord, and each one is saved. We don't just fling our prayers out into the vastness of space, where they swirl around in oblivion. No, they are heard immediately by our gracious, caring, heavenly Father.

> *We don't just fling our prayers out into the vastness of space, where they swirl around in oblivion. No, they are heard immediately by our gracious, caring, heavenly Father.*

He is touched by our prayers and takes each and every one seriously and answers them. Sometimes the answer is a yes, sometimes a no, and sometimes "wait." But He always answers.

Why Pray?

As we pray, many benefits come to us in addition to seeing answers. Why should we pray?

> Because it's fellowshipping with our heavenly Father (Revelation 3:20).

Because prayer gives God glory (John 14:13).

Because prayer saves us out of all our troubles (Psalm 34:6).

Because we can know God's wisdom (James 1:5).

Because prayer defeats Satan (Matthew 18:18–20).

Because faith is increased (James 5:17–18).

Because prayer brings results (James 5:16; Matthew 6:10).

Because Jesus prayed (Mark 1:35).

As God's children we must be about our highest calling—prayer. Therefore, no matter what, let me encourage you to be disciplined in the practice of prayer, praying when you feel like it and when you don't. Be aware that at times your prayers will seem dull and unreal. Author E. Stanley Jones explains it as "the glow" not being there. He encourages us by saying, "Hold steady, the glow will return. In doing so you will be fixing a prayer habit. You're being fashioned into a person who lives by principles rather than pulse-beats, by decision rather than by delights. Prayer is always right, with or without an emotional content."[2]

Talking with our Father gives us the opportunity to experience His presence, allowing Him to touch us at our deepest levels of need. This chapter has given you an introduction in how to talk to God using each of the four steps—praise, confession, thanksgiving, and intercession— to shape your prayers. In the next part of the book, we'll take a closer look at each of those steps, practice each step, and begin the adventure of discovering just how life-changing prayer can be.

> *Heavenly Father, thank You for desiring an intimate relationship with me. Help me to settle in my mind that I will find time to be with You. Remind me of the lasting benefits of fellowship with You and of the difference praying can make in my life and the lives of my loved ones. May this passage from the Psalms reflect my heart: "Whom have I in heaven but you? And earth has nothing I desire besides you. My flesh and my heart may fail, but God is the strength of my heart and my portion forever.... But as for me, it is good to be near God. I have made the Sovereign LORD my refuge." In Jesus' name, amen.*

Part 2

Praying the Four Steps

4. Praise: Praying According to God's Attributes

A kindergarten teacher was observing her classroom of children while they drew. Occasionally she would walk around to see each child's artwork. As she watched one little girl who was working diligently, the teacher asked what her drawing was. The little girl replied, "I'm drawing God." The teacher paused and said, "But no one knows what God looks like." Without missing a beat or looking up from her drawing, the girl replied, "They will in a minute."

Wouldn't you love to have seen her drawing? Fortunately for us, throughout Scripture God has painted a portrait of Himself by revealing His character. We can know what He "looks" like through learning and studying His attributes (an attribute is a quality God has revealed about Himself). His portrait never conflicts with itself; He is who He says He is. As we get to know Him, we'll have an increasing desire to exalt, adore, and esteem Him—and to make His portrait known.

Jack R. Taylor in his book *The Hallelujah Factor* sums it up this way, "Praise is nothing more or less than a commitment to, and a confession of, the sovereign power and providence of God.... To know Him is to praise Him."[1] When we praise Him, we join a chorus of millions, for the Psalms say, "Thy saints shall bless thee" (Psalm 145:10, KJV).

Praise is a lifelong, treasure-finding journey of getting to know our God. It's distinguished from thanksgiving in that praise is worshiping God for who He is while thanksgiving is centered on what He has done.

No requests are made during this opening step in our praying. Author Dick Eastman states, "We must first draw our attention to God in prayer before we draw our attention to self.... In its very nature, praise is unselfish."[2]

Praising God at the outset of our prayer time puts Him in His rightful position, giving a throne-room perspective that a loving, sovereign God is in control. The truth of His attributes gives the firm foundation from which our intercessions will flow later. This is a sacred time that encourages us to focus on what is true and unchanging about God rather than concentrating on changing circumstances.

Closer to God

Before I instituted the idea of using the four steps of prayer into my quiet time, my prayers consisted mostly of confessions and requests. But now I start with praise. As a result, I continue to learn more about Him, experiencing a wonderful awareness of His loving presence.

I hear from moms all over the world how praising God has brought them into a deeper, more intimate relationship with Him. Lynna wrote, "As I prepared for our prayer group's hour of prayer, I learned so much about the attributes and character of our Lord. It was several years before I realized that each time I researched those attributes for our group, I was learning more about Him. And that the more I knew about Him, the more my relationship with Him became personal."

What part of your prayer life consists of praising the Lord for who He is? It might help you to incorporate praise into your prayers by remembering that we all like to be praised. Within each of us is the desire to be valued, admired, and honored for our virtues or accomplishments. But how much more our heavenly Father deserves recognition and admiration. He is the One who is righteous in all His ways (Psalm 145:17), absolutely sinless, without a single flaw. The psalmist said, "Not to us, O LORD, not to us but to your name be the glory, because of your love and faithfulness" (Psalm 115:1). When we glorify Him, we stand in awe of His holiness, are comforted by His sovereign kingship, rejoice in His boundless omniscience, and are blessed by His matchless grace and love.

What does one do during a praise time? I've found using Scripture has been my best teacher. In the Psalms, David expresses his love and adoration to the Lord so eloquently. He always seems to uncover an amazing facet of God's nature. As I read his words, I offer them back to God from my own heart, praying, "Heavenly Father, You are 'gracious and compassionate, slow to anger and rich in love. You are good to all; You have compassion on all You have made'" (Psalm 145:8–9).

Other times I might choose an attribute, such as faithfulness. I look up verses on faithfulness in the concordance from the back of my Bible or from the attribute sheets from Moms In Touch. Out of these verses a prayer emerges. "O, Lord, great and unrivaled is Your faithfulness. Faithfulness defines Your very character. You are faithful in all things and at all times. Your ways are perfect, and Your promises are sure. I exalt You that what You have said You will accomplish. There is never the slightest deviation in Your faithfulness. You do not change, and Your mercies and compassion never fail. You are faithful to provide all that I need. It is with great praise and adoration I esteem You as my faithful God."

> *When we glorify Him, we stand in awe of His holiness, are comforted by His sovereign kingship, rejoice in His boundless omniscience, and are blessed by His matchless grace and love.*

Praise can be as simple as declaring, "Lord, You are faithful," "Lord, You are holy," or "Father, You are loving."

Other Sources for Praise

In addition to drawing from Scripture, I love to glean from the saints. Reading classics such as Oswald Chambers, E. M. Bounds, and Charles Spurgeon focuses me on so many praiseworthy aspects of our Lord and expresses them in language that lifts me right up to the heavenlies. You might have other favorites or more contemporary writers such as Dick Eastman or Max Lucado.

Charles Spurgeon ignites our hearts to praise God for His goodness when he writes, "His goodness is seen in creation. It shines in every sunbeam, glitters in every dewdrop, smiles in every flower, and whispers in every breeze. Earth and sea and air, teeming with innumerable forms of life, are all full of the goodness of the Lord. Sun, moon, and stars affirm that the Lord is good, and all terrestrial things echo the proclamation."[3]

Wow! Can we all say together a hearty "Amen, praise the Lord"? The more we learn to actually praise God, the more natural it becomes.

Another wonderful way to praise Him is to speak or sing the old hymns. Here is one of my favorites, "O the Deep, Deep Love of Jesus."

O the deep, deep love of Jesus,
Vast, unmeasured, boundless, free!
Rolling as a mighty ocean
In its fullness over me,
Underneath me, all around me,
Is the current of Thy love;
Leading onward, leading homeward
To my glorious rest above.

O the deep, deep love of Jesus,
Spread His praise from shore to shore!
How He loveth, ever loveth,
Changeth never, nevermore;
How He watches o'er His loved ones,
Died to call them all His own;
How for them He intercedeth,
Watcheth o'er them from the throne.

Samuel Trevor Francis

The Comfort His Attributes Bring

If we pursue the goal of praising God every day, we will find that for every need, problem, inadequacy, or trial we encounter, some attribute wells up in our hearts, giving us the peace and strength to be victorious in the situation.

One mom found praising God brought her through the heartache she experienced over her daughter. She tells her story this way:

"Our fifteen-year-old daughter, Marci, didn't return home from work one night. She had chosen to leave home for a life of 'freedom' with a friend who had no boundaries. This choice fed into our daughter's immoral lifestyle and drinking problem. The day after she left home, my Moms In Touch group was meeting. Our praise that day was 'The Lord is our keeper.' Psalm 145 tells us that the Lord watches over all who love Him, but all the wicked, He will destroy. I praised God for this attribute, knowing He was keeping my emotions intact and keeping my daughter's life from harm. During our intercession time, we prayed Psalm 121:7 for my daughter, putting her name in the Scripture: 'The Lord will keep [Marci] from all harm—he will watch over [Marci's] life; the Lord will watch over [Marci's] coming and going both now and forevermore.' God was her keeper through the next four years of wrong choices, all the while encouraging me from His Word. Eventually she returned home, and the closeness that was stolen in her teenage years returned in her twenties. This summer, twelve years later, her father and I stood alongside her as she married the man whom we had prayed for—on our thirty-fourth wedding anniversary. Yes, God is our keeper—so faithful to hear and answer every prayer on our children's behalf as we wait on Him."

Often in the difficulties of life we come to know God better. He draws us to Himself through praise. As Spurgeon states,

> It is in the storm that we learn to "praise the LORD for His goodness and for His wonderful works to the children of men" (Psalm 107:8). If I might have it so, I could wish my whole life to be as calm as a fair summer's evening when scarcely a breeze stirs the happy flowers. I could desire that nothing might again disturb the serenity of my restful spirit. . . . Doubtless it is that we would not perceive the greatness of goodness if we did not see the depth of the horrible pit from which it snatches us.[4]

No, we wouldn't choose to have storms, but what we will find in the storm is God, who changes our fears to faith.

Rle and I experienced a fearful situation when our son Troy was three years old. One morning I bundled up Troy and drove to the clinic, thinking he might have tonsillitis. As the doctor finished his examination, I noticed he looked concerned. He said that he felt an enlargement in Troy's abdominal area. Confused by what he felt, he called for another doctor to examine Troy. They thought something might be wrong with his spleen but weren't sure. After conferring, they agreed that X rays were needed.

In what seemed like a blur, Troy and I were on our way to the X-ray room. The X rays showed an obstruction in his right kidney, and his left kidney was filling with poisonous fluids. What was just a normal doctor's visit became a storm.

The next weeks were a whirlwind of tests and visits to the doctors. The decision was made: The left kidney had to be removed; the right one was to be left alone.

The day of the operation arrived. A huge lump had settled in my throat, and tears welled up as the medical staff rolled Troy away on the gurney. I felt so powerless. I could no longer touch him, console him, pray with him, sing to him. I was forced to release his little life into God's hands.

As I ran to God, His attribute that changed my fear to faith was that He was Creator. He created Troy just the way he was. Never before did that truth resonate so deeply in my heart.

I sat in the waiting room for three hours, pouring over the Word of God. Hungering to hear Him speak to my anxious heart, I filled my mind with praises for God the Creator. Placing Troy's name in Psalm 139:13–16 (TLB), I prayed, "Father, I praise You that You created Troy. You made all the delicate, inner parts of his body and knit them together in my womb. Thank You for making Troy so wonderfully complex! It is amazing to think about. Your workmanship is marvelous—and how well I know it. You were there while Troy was being formed in utter seclusion! You saw him before he was born and scheduled each day of his life before he began to breathe. Every day was recorded in Your Book!"

Something happened to my spirit as I praised God the Creator. God's peace covered my heart like a warm blanket. I can testify that if we acquaint ourselves with God, we will be at peace (Job 22:21). Other Scriptures comforted my heart during that time, and I continued to offer my praise. The more I praised Him, the easier it was for me to rest. I relinquished my son into my Father's arms.

During that trying time God brought to mind a verse that powerfully touched me. "I need not fear Someone who loves [Troy] perfectly; for his perfect love for [Troy] eliminates all dread of what he might do to [Troy]. And if [I am] afraid, it is for fear of what he might do to [Troy], and shows that [I am] not fully convinced that he really loves [Troy]" (1 John 4:18, TLB).

Through many answered prayers, the left kidney was removed without complications. Every six months we had his right kidney checked to make sure the obstruction wasn't worsening. God in His grace and divine purposes for Troy healed the remaining kidney. He is now thirty-one years old, and that kidney is functioning fine.

Something happened to my spirit as I praised God the Creator. God's peace covered my heart like a warm blanket.

Choosing to give praise helped me to take my eyes off the circumstances and to put them on God, to move from seeing the battle to gazing on the Victor. As Jehoshaphat said, "We do not know what to do, but our eyes are upon you" (2 Chronicles 20:12).

We know that in life we will face trouble, fear, anxiety, sickness, loneliness, emptiness, abandonment, vulnerability, heartache. When it hits you, what are you going to do? Will you be "practiced" in offering praise to our Lord?

I have many friends right now who are in heart-wrenching trials. One mom is despondent over a rebellious daughter who is addicted to drugs and is in jail. Another woman has just heard the devastating news that her husband is leaving her. A family is trying to emotionally survive their son's fatal accident. A husband's sudden death has devastated his wife. A mom of four young daughters has cancer in her ear and brain. Yes, living on planet Earth brings tribulation.

The Benefits of Praise

How good of God to command us to praise Him. It not only brings Him glory but it also benefits us.

Little did Doreen Tomlin know that God was going to ask her to give a "sacrifice of praise" (Jeremiah 17:26b, KJV). As Joni Eareckson Tada explains, "Sometimes our gift of praise involves cost, for praising in the midst of suffering makes praise all the more glorious."

Doreen's son, John, was one of the students killed at Columbine High School. How does a mother endure such a loss? What words could possibly comfort her shattered heart?

I asked her what helped her through that difficult time. She said, "Like a cat claws a tree, I clung to God's attributes with a passion. But the attribute that has meant the most to me is God's omniscience." (His knowledge of everything.)

At times she found herself ruminating on the "what ifs." *What if we hadn't moved to Littleton? What if we would have sent him to another school?* But her thoughts never spun out of control because she had established the practice over ten years of praising God for His attributes.

She found solace in these Scriptures: "Oh, the depth of the riches of the wisdom and *knowledge* of God! How unsearchable are his judgments, and his paths beyond tracing out!" "*Known* unto God are all his works from the beginning of the world." "For I *know* the plans I have for you." "How precious to me are your thoughts, O God! How vast is the sum of them!" (Romans 11:33; Acts 15:18; Jeremiah 29:11; Psalm 139:17, italics mine).

God brought Doreen face-to-face with His omniscience, including His knowledge of what would happen to her son. She chose to trust her God who knows everything—all events—past, present, and future. Praise helped overrule her sorrow and gave her peace even through her weeping, causing her praise to be "all the more glorious"!

Let's Pray

Praise is a powerful time of prayer when God's name, His attributes, and His character are worshiped. Learning to praise your God will draw you into a sweet, intimate relationship with Him. He longs to reveal Himself to you through praise.

How to Praise:

1. *Choose one attribute.* (A list of attributes and accompanying Scripture are provided on pages 189–193. A Praise Quiet Time Sheet is also provided on page 194 to help direct you through your prayer time.) Let's use God's omniscience as our example.

2. *Look up the definition of the attribute in a dictionary or thesaurus.* "Omniscient: having infinite knowledge, knowing all things, having universal knowledge, all-seeing."

3. *Find Scripture that talks about the attribute.* You could use the concordance in the back of your Bible to help you locate passages, or turn to a list of Scripture at the back of this book on pages 189–193.

4. *Read the Scripture.* Romans 11:33 talks about God's omniscience. "Oh, the depth of the riches of the wisdom and knowledge of God! How unsearchable his judgments, and his paths beyond tracing out!"

5. *Pray the Scripture back to God as a praise. Praise Him for what He has revealed to you about Himself.* "Heavenly Father, I marvel at the depth of Your wisdom. Your knowledge is so rich and deep that it's beyond comprehension. You know all things, and You know them instantaneously. I praise You that there is nothing You do not know. I rejoice that in Your supreme wisdom the outcome of each situation is always for my best possible good. Your wisdom truly is too wonderful for me to comprehend. I don't understand Your ways, but I trust Your heart. I praise You that You are my all-knowing God. In Your Son's name, amen."

6. *Find another passage to pray through.* You are getting to know your God.

Dispelling Power, Destroying Lies

Satan doesn't want us to have victory in devastating circumstances. He wants us to doubt God's love. He works hard at trying to undermine our concept of who God is. If he can succeed, we are left weak, fearful, and unbelieving. That's why it's so important to know God. Giving God praise actually dispels Satan's power. When we speak truth, addressing God for who He is, our prayer destroys Satan's lies. If we believe his lies, they can destroy us. "Praise ... promptly sends Satan running," says author Dick Eastman. "He cannot tolerate the presence of God. Where do we find God's presence? In Psalm 22:3 we are reminded that God inhabits 'the praises' of His people."[5]

To develop a praise life is to develop immunity to the enemy's attacks. Paul Billheimer further suggests, "Satan is allergic to praise, so where there is massive triumphant praise, Satan is paralyzed, bound, and banished."[6] After all, that's what Jesus did in Matthew 4:8–10. When He was tempted, He responded by saying, "Away from me, Satan! For it is written: 'Worship the Lord your God, and serve him only.'"

King Jehoshaphat was in a horrific situation. Three armies were on their way to make war against the people of Judah. After King Jehoshaphat sought his God and consulted with godly leaders, the plan was laid. Judah would defeat the enemy through praise. The choir would lead the march, "clothed in sanctified garments and singing the song, 'His Loving-kindness Is Forever'" (2 Chronicles 20:21, TLB). The choir? Praise? Walking in front of the army?

Listen to what happened: "And at the moment they began to sing and to praise, the Lord caused the armies of Ammon, Moab, and Mount Seir to begin fighting among themselves, and they destroyed each other!" (2 Chronicles 20:22, TLB). God intervenes mightily when we praise, dispelling Satan's power and providing victory.

The enemy wanted to attack Marlae's faith as she faced what seemed like an impossible situation with her daughter. "In the summer of 1999, my husband and I put our seventeen-year-old daughter on an airplane bound for her aunt's home 2,500 miles away. Our daughter was in big trouble, making wrong choices and hanging around with a rough crowd. Through counsel and much prayer, God led us to send her away from us, hoping and praying that the distance and tough love would speak to her heart. I can still remember the heaviness of my heart.

"In many ways, it should have been the worst summer of my life, but as I look back, I think it was the best. Each morning that summer, I made a choice to focus on one of God's attributes. I experienced His peace and faithfulness like I never had before. He taught me that, as long as I looked up to Him and reminded myself daily (sometimes hourly) that He was constant, He was there, and He was faithful, I could and would get through it."

Nothing is as powerful as praise. Praise gives glory due His name; draws us more intimately to the Father's heart; causes us to look up— setting our minds on things above; changes our attitude; brings an awareness of God's presence; defeats Satan; releases God's power; brings a victorious perspective; provides peace; wards off the spirits of self-pity, depression, and discouragement; and produces strength in an anxious heart. Through praise we find hope in what seems like impossible situations. Let us praise the Lord's name.

"Blessed are those who have learned to acclaim you, who walk in the light of your presence, O LORD. They rejoice in your name all day long; they exult in your righteousness" (Psalm 89:15–16).

> *O Lord God Almighty, I pray for an outpouring of Your Holy Spirit on me, that the eyes of my heart would be enlightened to know You through the power of praise. Give me a heart of praise, worshiping You with a pure heart. May I seek You with all my heart and find the sweet awareness of Your presence. I pray the prayer of A. W. Tozer: "Prophet and psalmist, apostle and saint have encouraged me to believe that I may in some measure know Thee. Therefore, I pray, whatever of Thyself Thou hast been pleased to disclose, help me to search out as treasure more precious than rubies or the merchandise of fine gold."[7] Amen.*

5. Confession: Removing Rubble

Linda was a Bible college graduate, yet she felt something was missing in her walk with the Lord. "I didn't know what it was," she said, "just that something wasn't right." Then, after hearing a speaker talk about confession at a retreat, a bright light went on for Linda. "I realized I never had learned how to deal with sin. I was knowledgeable about God and the Bible, but somehow I missed out on understanding that whenever we know we are in sin we need to give it up at that moment."

In the past, Linda had saved up the items she needed to confess until the end of the day or the weekend or whenever she had time to get to it. "Of course, I often forgot areas I needed to confess once I made time to bring my sins before the Lord," Linda remarked. "I had quite a collection to take care of, but praise the Lord, I now know what to do—and to do it right away."

What about you? Do you know what to do with the offenses you commit against God? Do they collect in a heap inside your heart until you feel too unworthy to even pray? And what about the sins you consider really big? Do you know how to bring them to God to receive a clean heart?

A woman told me that as a result of learning how to confess her sin, for the first time she felt truly forgiven. When she was seventeen she had an abortion, but despite asking forgiveness over and over, she never could let go of the choice she had made. Even though she had a loving husband and two beautiful children, she still felt guilt.

Then, after hearing a talk on forgiveness and confession, she said, "I couldn't think of anyone in my life I needed to forgive. Then I realized it was me I needed to forgive. I feel like a huge weight has been lifted off. That talk led me to God's loving heart."

Whether our sins are everyday acts and thoughts that need to be brought before the Lord or areas of guilt we've harbored in our hearts for years, having a regular time of confession helps to cleanse us and enables us to freely communicate with God. That's why, in our four-step prayer process, we follow our time of praise with a time of confession.

Becoming a Clean Vessel

To pray effectively and with power, we must be clean vessels. During this time ask the Holy Spirit to reveal anything that keeps you from a vital relationship with Jesus and from having a powerful prayer life.

Dick Eastman in his book *The Hour That Changes the World* says, "According to Scripture there can be no effective prayer life where sin maintains its grip in the life of the believer. This is why confession is critical to our praying and should be implemented early in prayer."[1]

Michelle wanted her personal relationship with Jesus to be vibrant and close; so she got serious about those things that were keeping her from experiencing all that God wanted her to be. As she tells it, "How can I best describe what happened to me as I listened to a speaker at a retreat? I asked myself questions: What's dead in my walk with the Lord that needs to blossom again? What about my sensitivity to sin? Ouch! Did that ever pierce my heart. Jesus' blood doesn't cleanse excuses but cleanses confessed sin. Some thought-provoking questions were asked: Am I known for my unselfishness? My thoughtfulness? My patience? My forgiveness?

"So in a private confession time, I sat on a rock in sunny San Diego and gave up my control. I gave up 'my way'—my self-confidence, my unforgiveness, my impatience, and my selfishness. I confessed them, and Jesus lifted a huge burden. I tore up the paper on which I had listed my sins and over the top of the list had written, 'His blood was shed for these.'

"I feel new. I feel refreshed and refined like I've come through the fire. I have never cried so many tears; it felt so good. I've wanted this for so long."

Removing the Rubble

Nehemiah was called by God to motivate, challenge, and lead the children of Israel to rebuild Jerusalem's wall after its enemies had invaded the city and dismantled its encircling wall. The task was monumental. Nehemiah observed that the strength of the workers was giving out, and so much rubble lay about they couldn't rebuild the wall (Nehemiah 4:10).

What was the rubble? The broken pieces of stone that once formed the wall around Jerusalem. The rubble had to be discarded before the wall could be rebuilt.

Like Michelle, for us to grow in our relationship with the Lord we must remove the rubble—the sin that incapacitates us, depriving us of the motivation to move forward in our walk with Christ. Sin breaks our fellowship with God. It blocks our communion with Jesus.

And Satan couldn't be happier than when that happens. He is the enemy of our souls and does everything in his power to separate us from the Beloved and to keep us in a prayerless state. Sin also keeps us from an effective ministry to our families and others. It robs us of Christ's power and joy. The debris in our lives keeps us from full surrender, and we often find ourselves dry, unyielding, lifeless, and sometimes numb, uncaring, and maybe even depressed. Unconfessed sin brings shame, self-debasement, and prolonged guilt (Psalm 32:3–4).

Set Free from Destruction

As God's children, we are set free from sin's destruction through Jesus. It cost God the life of His Son to satisfy His wrath against sin. We need to remind ourselves that as God's children, our position before Him is holy. He no longer sees my sin or yours; He sees Jesus' blood that took away all our sin, and we stand before Him holy. I love the promise in 2 Corinthians 5:21: "For God took the sinless Christ and poured into him our sins. Then, in exchange, he poured God's goodness into us" (TLB).

Your position means you always will be His child. You were given a new nature at the moment of your salvation experience (2 Corinthians 5:17). But you still have your old nature. And the two natures war against one another. Throughout each day you must make choices, whether you're going to let Christ rule in your heart or let self rule. Therefore, your "condition" at any given moment can be Christ-like or self-like.

For Christ to reign in your life, you must deal with daily sins. Now, that doesn't mean at night you lie in bed thinking back through the day if you sinned. It means that in the split second when the Holy Spirit convicts you of sin, you confess it. Agree with God that what you did or said was wrong, admit that you sinned.

The moment the Holy Spirit convicts you of sin, you need to deal with it. Author Jennifer Kennedy Dean calls these "crucifixion moments." In these painful but important moments, you decide to react in the way of the Spirit. "When you choose to place blame on others or feel martyred by circumstances beyond your control," Dean continues, "you resuscitate your self-life. On the other hand, if you choose to look away from the outside cause and accept the crucifying work of the Spirit, you begin, little by little, to let the old nature die and the new nature emerge."[2]

Along with confession, you also must repent. Joy Dawson in her book *Intimate Friendship with God* explains it so well. "We can confess sin, shed tears of remorse, and weep over the mess it has gotten us into, but we may never really repent of it. Repentance means a change of mind, a change of heart, and a change of life toward sin."[3]

Just agreeing with God that you have sinned but then not repenting of sin produces no lasting change. Paul confirms this in Acts 26:20: "That they should repent and turn to God and prove their repentance by their deeds." Change will take place if confession is sincere.

When we fail to respond to the Holy Spirit's conviction concerning our sin, we can't hear the requests that God wants to lay upon our hearts. Many times I've repented of my sin so that my heart would be receptive to hear from God how to pray for my children. God knows when they need immediate prayer. They could be facing temptation or physical harm or need wisdom in a difficult situation. But I must be a clean channel for the Holy Spirit to place upon my heart whom to pray for and how to pray.

I wonder how many opportunities to make a difference in people's lives are missed because we hold onto our sin, not dealing with it immediately. And I wonder how many of our prayers aren't heard because we haven't cleaned out the rubble. Isaiah 59:1–2 states, "Surely the arm of the LORD is not too short to save, nor his ear too dull to hear. But your iniquities have separated you from your God; your sins have hidden his face from you, so that he will not hear."

Separated from Jesus

Sin not only keeps us from an active, fruitful prayer life but also hinders our communion with Jesus. I certainly have found that true.

One morning the day seemed to be starting out well. I had planned that after the children left for school, I would spend a good portion of the morning with the Lord. I anticipated a sweet time, desiring to hear from my Father as well as give Him my burdens.

But wouldn't you know it? That very morning Rle and I had a disagreement. I don't even remember what the tiff was about, but I was irritated with him and he with me. When Rle and I are at odds, we don't throw things or raise our voices; we just don't talk. So the temperature in the house reaches freezing. Icicles hang everywhere. On this particular morning, I didn't know what to do. I wanted to spend time with my holy Father yet I had these icy feelings toward Rle. I thought I should say a few civil words to him before he left for work.

"Have a good day," I tossed out and headed to my bedroom to have an intimate time with Jesus. As I opened the Bible, I prayed Psalm 119:18, "Open my eyes that I may see wonderful things in your law."

The Father spoke conviction to my heart. "Fern, what are you doing?"

"Oh, Father, I can't wait for You to reveal nuggets from Your Word this morning."

"But, what about Rle?"

"What about Rle?" I knew where this was headed.

"You know, that man you don't like very much right now. That man you have ill feelings toward."

I proceeded to tell the Lord my side. I've learned you might as well tell Him what you're thinking because He knows it anyway. "Lord, You saw the whole thing. If he hadn't said what he did, then I wouldn't have reacted the way I did. Maybe I was one percent wrong, but he was ninety-nine percent wrong."

Then the Lord said, "Fern, your salvation was separate from your husband's and so is your walk. What you perceive as your one percent is what you need to call Rle about and ask forgiveness for."

Oh my, did my two natures have a battle. I didn't want to call Rle, yet I knew that fellowship was broken. First Samuel 15:22 says that to obey is better than to sacrifice. God wanted my obedience.

I had tried partial obedience. After all, I did say kind words when Rle left for work. But God wanted full obedience. What did that mean? In Matthew 5, God tells us what we should do. "If you are offering your gift at the altar and there remember that your brother has something against you, leave your gift there in front of the altar. First go and be reconciled to your brother; then come and offer your gift. Settle matters quickly with your adversary" (vv. 23–25).

Would I die to self, to my pride, and be obedient to the Word even if I didn't feel like it? Isn't it astounding to think God would forfeit His communion with us because of His desire to see His children love each other? He says that "if we walk in the light, as he is in the light, we have fellowship with one another, and the blood of Jesus, his Son, purifies us from all sin" (1 John 1:7). A good test of whether we are walking in the light is how we are walking with others.

I sat there thinking, *How am I going to ask Rle to forgive me without saying, "Will you forgive me?"* Nothing came to mind. Those were hard words. I came face-to-face with my pride. "Lord, help me," I cried. "I can't do this. Only Jesus can. I want to die to self, but it is so hard. By the power of Your Spirit in me, help me to do the right thing."

Out of obedience, not with warm, fuzzy emotions, I called Rle. "Rle, will you forgive me for my bad attitude this morning?" Already I was feeling better. Pride was taking a backseat, and humility was driving.

Rle readily forgave me and then asked for my forgiveness. Now, I have to admit at that moment the thought came to me, *Well, why didn't you call me first?* Refusing to linger on that question, I said, "Good-bye. I love you," and was free. Free from guilt. Self was dealt a blow by admitting my sin and making it right with Rle. I was in the light. The Holy Spirit now was at liberty to reveal truth from the Word to a heart that was free from rubble.

Freeing Others

In Matthew 18:21–22, Jesus gives a spine-chilling account of what happens to people who don't forgive. Peter asks the Lord how many times he should forgive his brother who has sinned against him. Peter thought he was being generous when he suggested "up to seven times" because that was four more than the religious leaders of that day would say.

I can't imagine how startled Peter must have been when Jesus said, "I do not say to you, up to seven times, but up to seventy times seven" (NASB). In other words, so many times that you can't keep count— without limits—as many times as it takes.

Then Jesus proceeded to tell a story. A king threatened to imprison a servant who owed him millions of dollars. The servant fell to his knees before the king and pleaded, "Be patient with me, and I will pay back everything." The servant's master took pity on him, canceled the debt, and let him go. Then the servant ran out and immediately found a fellow servant who owed him a few dollars, grabbed him by the neck and demanded, "Pay up!" He ignored the man's pleas for mercy but had him thrown into prison until he could pay back the tiny debt.[4]

When the king heard of this great injustice, he had the unmerciful servant brought before him. He said, "You wicked servant, I canceled all your debt because you begged me to. Shouldn't you have had mercy on your fellow servant just as I had on you?"

We could all shout "Amen" right here, agreeing with the king's justice. After all, how could this servant do such a horrible thing, especially since he had been forgiven so much?

But I wonder, are you and I guilty of the same offense? What was Jesus saying? You've been forgiven a great debt. In God's mercy, all your sins were paid for at Calvary. Actually, no greater debt has ever been paid than the sins of the whole world. What a great forgiveness! You must do the same and give others mercy, even if they don't deserve it. David Daniels says it this way: "Our sin is enormous, incalculable. Others' sins against me are minuscule compared to my sin against God. So forgiving my debtors should be an overflow of the forgiveness I have already received from the Lord."[5]

Now, let's take a look at the consequences, according to Matthew 18, if we refuse to forgive, to clean out the rubble in our hearts. The king had the servant "turned ... over to the jailers to be tortured, until he should pay back all he owed" (verse 34). Tormentors! That's pretty strong language and pretty tough consequences. What does it mean? Speaker Bill Gothard says, "Tormentors are destructive emotions such as depression, fear, worry, and anger, which are allowed by God to bring us to repentance until we would learn to forgive."[6]

Isn't that true? The person you hate, the one you won't forgive, the one who has hurt you so terribly that you feel the relationship is beyond repair, is the person you constantly think about. That person controls you. You rehearse the incident, the whole terrible scenario, over and over again. If you won't forgive, you put yourself in the torture chamber of destructive emotions.

The psalmist tells us the consequence of rebelling against His Word. "Some sat in darkness and the deepest gloom, prisoners suffering in iron chains, for they had rebelled against the words of God and despised the counsel of the Most High" (Psalm 107:10–11). None of us wants to be there!

What must we do? Psalm 107:13–14 says, "Then they cried to the LORD in their trouble, and he saved them from their distress. He brought them out of darkness and the deepest gloom and broke away their chains."

Do you have chains that need to be broken? Whom have you shackled yourself to? Cry out to God and admit to Him your unforgiving spirit. Name the sin. Is it bitterness, hatred, condemnation? Say it. Get it out in the open so you can see the sin as God sees it. Then claim the blood of Jesus Christ. Forgiveness is through the blood. It washes as white as snow. As the old hymn declares, "What can wash away my sin? Nothing but the blood of Jesus. What can make me whole again? Nothing but the blood of Jesus."

Then repent of the sin and ask God to fill you with His Holy Spirit. Thank God that He has forgiven you according to the promise of 1 John 1:9: "If we confess our sins, He is faithful and righteous to forgive us our sins and to cleanse us from all unrighteousness" (NASB).

Freeing Your Heart from Resentment

One of the greatest struggles a woman has is not to harbor anger and resentment against her husband. In such a close relationship, a sense of betrayal can readily settle in. But that can lead to harboring sin. I've learned to immediately pray for Rle when I feel resentment toward him. That's not been easy to come to and has taken determination on my part, but it's enabled us to be in such a place of closeness and keeps my heart from harboring sinful emotions.

In marriage, as my incident with Rle illustrates, one of the hardest tasks is to forgive your partner. That's especially true when you see no change in behavior or attitude. True forgiveness lets incidents go and keeps your heart clean before the Lord. That's love at its finest. It's the love 1 Corinthians 13 talks about. "Love is patient, love is kind. It does not envy, it does not boast, it is not proud. It is not rude, it is not self-seeking, it is not easily angered, *it keeps no record of wrongs*" (vv. 5–6, italics mine).

You know you are to love your husband and yet you find yourself tolerating him. You might protest, "That's easy for you to say, but you don't know my husband! You don't know what I've been through." The Lord does, and He cares; yet He tells you that you are to respect your husband, be his helpmate, his supporter, his encourager. He wants to free you from sin, bondage, and guilt to be all these things to your husband. (Obviously, in an abusive situation, the circumstances are very different, and action to protect yourself might very well be necessary.)

How can we restore love for our husbands? Old, sinful thinking habits must be replaced with new. I know of no better way than to use God's Word. Whenever you're tempted to think critical, unkind, belittling thoughts, pray for your husband. Romans 12:2 says, "Do not conform any longer to the pattern of this world, but be transformed by the renewing of your mind." The best way to transform your mind, to keep from sinning, is to fill your thoughts with the Word by memorizing it. The psalmist testifies, "I have hidden your word in my heart that I might not sin against you" (Psalm 119:11). When we sin, it is against God. David expresses this truth in Psalm 51:4 when he confesses his adulterous relationship with Bathsheba. "Against you [God], you only, have I sinned and done what is evil in your sight."

I recommend memorizing and praying Colossians 1:9–11 for your husband:

Heavenly Father, I ask that You fill (place your husband's name here) with the knowledge of Your will through all spiritual wisdom and understanding. I ask this that he might live a life worthy of You and might please You in every way, bearing fruit in every good work, growing in the knowledge of You. I pray that You would strengthen him with all power according to Your glorious might so that he may have great endurance and patience.

Making this a discipline will change your unclean heart to a heart like God's. You will begin to see your husband as God sees him and love him as God loves him. Don't be discouraged if this doesn't happen overnight. God in His faithfulness will change you little by little, as you are obedient.

I want to give you one last encouragement concerning someone who has hurt you deeply. Ask God right now if you have unresolved issues with someone who has hurt you. Who comes to mind? How do you feel when you think about that person? It might be someone who has maligned your name, falsely accused you. You are the wounded party, the one wronged. Words can hurt so deeply, and you can remember them for years. So what do you do with this hurt?

Several years ago I found myself in such a situation. I had no idea what I was about to face as I entered a room for a scheduled meeting. A prominent Christian leader whom I admired, loved, and respected hurled false accusations—unfounded statements—at me. I felt devastated. My stomach churned and my heart pounded. Where did this false information come from?

Not knowing what to do, I prayed a quick prayer. "Help me, Father. I don't know what to do." He brought to mind the Scripture in which Jesus never opened His mouth when He was accused (Mark 14:61). I felt the Lord was asking me not to defend myself, not to say a thing, not to justify myself. That He would take care of it. I was silent. I left the meeting crushed, wounded, and hurting but at peace that I had done what God asked me to do.

After I returned home, I talked to the Lord about the situation. I didn't want to be bitter, and I didn't want Satan to get a foothold in my life and ministry nor in that of my accuser. I read 1 Peter 3:9: "Never return evil for evil or insult for insult—scolding, tongue-lashing, berating; but on the contrary blessing—praying for their welfare, happiness, and protection, and truly pitying and loving them. For know that to this you have been called, that you may yourself inherit a blessing (from God)—obtain a blessing as heirs, bringing welfare and happiness and protection" (AMP).

As an act of my will and by God's grace, I got on my knees and through many tears prayed for the accuser's happiness, welfare, and protection. At first, I had to pray this many times every day because my mind was consumed with the incident. I prayed that God would vindicate my name and that reconciliation would happen soon. As I prayed 1 Peter 3:9 day after day, the prayer became no longer just words of obedience. I experienced a flood of love as I prayed for the person who had uttered those words. The forgiveness had moved from my head into my heart. I really wanted happiness and success for that other person. And I realized that if that individual were holding a grudge against me, that person's prayer life and ministry would be hindered. I didn't want that. I wanted us to be reconciled. From that day on my prayers reflected a sincere love and desire for that person's happiness, welfare, and protection.

Many years later, my accuser "just happened" to be in a small prayer group with me. We were instructed to have a time of confession. This dear person began to ask God to forgive her for the accusations against me. She took up the allotted confession time to pour out her heart. No one in the group knew what she meant but me. After the prayer time, we hugged, and in my ear, she asked me if I could find it in my heart to forgive her. This was the moment I had prayed for. Because, years before, I was obedient to the Word, I could say to her, "I love you. I forgave you a long time ago."

Besetting Sins

But some of you might be thinking, *I seem to commit the same sin over and over again. It might not always be unforgiveness, but I have other sins that beset me, sins I can't seem to quit committing. I'm always having to confess that sin.*

Good, keep confessing, over and over. You might contend, "But doesn't the Lord get weary of my asking forgiveness for the same thing?" No, Jesus' blood keeps on cleansing. Regardless what the sin, new or old, the blood never stops flowing, covering current sins and all future sins. There is no sin that His blood doesn't wash clean, restoring fellowship to others and to God. His forgiveness is complete and is always available. If you stop dealing with the issue, that's when the rubble in your heart piles up, and your heart becomes cold and indifferent.

> *If you stop dealing with a sin, that's when the rubble in your heart piles up, and your heart becomes cold and indifferent.*

What besetting sin might you have? Overeating? Shopping to relieve stress or boredom? Gossiping? The sin itself might seem minor, but often it signals a deeper, more serious issue. I remember one time I was making my favorite cookies, chocolate chip. I struggle with self-control during cookie baking time. Actually, self-control can be nonexistent during this time. On this occasion I was determined to be good. But the gooey dough and the warm cookies just out of the oven were too much for me. I succumbed as I had many times before. After I ate my fill, I once again felt guilty. I had sinned. I went to the Father, discouraged over my failure and prayed, "Father, here I am again asking forgiveness for the sin of gluttony." It was as though He said to me, "'Again,' what do you mean 'again'?'

"Oh, You know, I've come to You many times concerning this."

"I don't know what you're talking about."

You see, what He was telling me was that each time I asked forgiveness, He forgave and remembered the sin no more (Hebrews 8:12). Just as He forgives me and doesn't bring it up again, He expects me to respond the same way with others.

How about you? Do you need to be reminded that God forgives you again and again? Or do you need to apply the truth of His generous forgiveness to someone in your life who needs to be forgiven over and over?

Remember, no matter how many times you have to ask forgiveness, God promises to forgive you. "If we confess our sins, He is faithful and righteous to forgive us our sins and to cleanse us from all unrighteousness" (1 John 1:9, NASB).

Each time we confess, we are forgiven, as this story by Ron Mehl illustrates so beautifully.

To a growing boy, there is nothing that sets the pulse racing like the winter's first major snow. We shaped armies of snowmen, constructed huge snow forts, waged violent snowball wars, ate homemade snow cones, and had more fun than ought to be legal.

With hundreds of neighborhood kids making snow angels, fighting pitched battles, marking off out-of-bounds lines for wild games of snow football, and generally trampling around on all the lawns and streets and vacant lots, it only took a few hours until there were no more areas of chaste, unsullied white. All the snow got used up, soiled, shoveled, scraped away, or frozen solid. The beautiful, pristine neighborhood we'd all seen out our windows in the morning began to look like an Arctic war zone or frosted gravel pit.

Not very much fun to play in anymore.

After searching in vain for virgin snow into the twilight hours, we had no choice but to go to bed tired—and a little sad—because of the mess we'd made of the once unblemished neighborhood.

But God was working the night shift.

When we woke the next morning, we beheld a wondrous thing. New snow. Fresh, beautiful snow. Lots and lots of it. An ocean of unbroken white.

All the forts, tunnels, broken snow persons, . . . and battle-fields were all covered almost as if they'd never been.

It was a brand new beginning. The past was the past.[7]

What a visual of confessed sin. We can certainly mess things up, and our hearts become soiled and ugly. But when we admit our sin, Jesus covers us with His blood like fresh snowfall. We have a new beginning.

Forgiving Yourself

By faith we believe that God has forgiven us, but sometimes, because of the ugliness of the sin and the consequences we have to live with, we have a hard time forgiving ourselves. Let's take a closer look at 1 John 1:9. Nothing is mentioned about sin's nature. Nothing is listed as such an awful sin that God will not forgive it. No mention is made of self-punishment. Nowhere does it say we only are forgiven if we didn't know what we were doing. The verse simply says, "If we confess . . . he is faithful to forgive."

If you confess your _____ (abortion, adultery, or whatever you think is too awful to be forgiven), He is faithful to forgive and cleanse. Don't be discouraged if you don't feel forgiven. We must not go by our feelings but by God's promise.

One woman who struggled to forgive herself made a cross and hammered it in the ground in her backyard. Every time Satan came against her to accuse her, she walked out the back door, pointed to the cross, and said, "I resist you, Satan. I am forgiven." She would walk away realizing, once again, that she was forgiven. She chose to believe God's truth rather than Satan's lies. There is such relief when guilt is gone. The psalmist proclaims, "Blessed is he whose transgressions are forgiven, whose sins are covered. Blessed is the man whose sin the LORD does not count against him and in whose spirit is no deceit" (Psalm 32:1–2).

To help you differentiate between God's call to clean up the rubble and Satan's call to feel guilty, just remember: Conviction is of God; condemnation is of Satan. God reveals the wrongdoing to set us *free* from the sin; Satan continually accuses and blames us to *bind* us within our sin.

Setting the Example

Confession of sin—cleaning up the rubble—is a wonderful legacy to pass down to our children. If they see us as proud, stiff-necked, and never admitting we're wrong, they will have those same tendencies.

> *Confession of sin—cleaning up the rubble—is a wonderful legacy to pass down to our children. If they see us as proud, stiff-necked, and never admitting we're wrong, they will have those same tendencies.*

I remember one time my son Travis and I had a disagreement. I hate it when we have unresolved feelings between us. So I said, "Lord, what should I do about this?" And I felt in my heart that God said, "You know, you really didn't listen to Travis. You make assumptions without finding out all the facts. You only heard what you wanted to hear."

So I went to Travis and asked him to forgive me for the things the Holy Spirit had convicted me of. He forgave me, and then there was healing. Fellowship was restored.

Not long after that we had another disagreement. Once again I asked the Lord if I needed to seek Travis's forgiveness. The Lord was

Let's Pray

1. **ASK** God to examine your heart to reveal areas that are not pleasing to Him. "Search me, O God, and know my heart; test me and know my anxious thoughts. See if there is any offensive way in me, and lead me in the way everlasting" (Psalm 139:23–24).

2. **WRITE** your sins on a sheet of paper as the Holy Spirit reveals them to you. (You may want to draw a cross on your paper to remind you that every sin you write down has been forgiven through the blood of Jesus Christ, who died for all your sins.)

3. **CONFESS** and **REPENT** concerning your sin. "Confess" means to agree with God regarding your sin. "Repent" means to turn away from these sins, to change your mind and heart toward the sins.

4. **WRITE** 1 John 1:9 over your list of sins as an expression of your believing God's promise concerning your sin: "If we confess our sins, he is faithful and just to forgive us our sins and to cleanse us from all unrighteousness" (KJV).

5. **THANK** God that He has forgiven you because of Christ's death on the cross. By giving thanks you are expressing that, by faith, you believe His word that you are forgiven.

6. **TEAR UP** the paper and throw it away! "For I will forgive their wickedness and will remember their sins no more" (Hebrews 8:12).

This exercise is to imprint on your heart and mind the once-and-for-all forgiveness. Guilt is gone! If you have confessed all known sin, any guilt remaining will be from Satan and not from God. Believe God's promise, not your feelings!

silent. I waited. That evening, on my pillow, I found a note. "Mom, we might not always see eye-to-eye, but we always see heart-to-heart. I love you. Travis."

I took that as my teenager's way of saying, "Will you forgive me?" Pride can raise its ugly head so easily, stealing the closeness that God wants for our families.

In Moms In Touch we pray that our children will recognize sin, confess it, and be willing to make restitution, if needed. Listen to this mother's story of answered prayer.

"I asked God to make my children's hearts sensitive to the Holy Spirit's guidance and correction, and I prayed according to several verses in Psalm 32 that they would have no deceit in their spirits (verse 2), that they would be quick to acknowledge sin, rather than to cover it up (verse 5), and that God would instruct and teach them in the way that they should go (verse 8).

"It wasn't long before Frances, my kindergartner, came to me with a long face. 'Mom,' she said, 'I lied to my teacher.' I stopped what I was doing and listened as her tale unfolded.

"Just before Christmas, the students had been invited to bring pennies to a classroom 'store,' where they could purchase little scraps of material, glitter, and other items to decorate their handmade Christmas trees. Frances had only brought one penny, but when she realized how hard it would be to decide between all the lovely items that were 'for sale,' she told the teacher that she had two cents to spend. Apparently no one ever checked to verify how much money each child actually had, so Frances's lie had gone undetected—and it had been eating her alive for months!

"'What do you think you should do?' I asked my little girl.

"'Well, I need to ask my teacher to forgive me, and I need to give her another penny,' she said slowly.

"I made an appointment for the two of us to talk to the teacher, who (thankfully!) understood the principle at work and took Frances's confession seriously, giving her a big hug as she accepted the penny from Frances's hand. I couldn't help but shed a little tear as I considered the tenderness of my daughter's heart and realized that God had answered my specific prayers from Psalm 32.

"Later that night, Frances snuggled up into my lap, her face a picture of contentment. 'I'm so glad I told my teacher what I did,' she said. 'Now I don't have to worry about it any more!'"

Is anything plaguing you? Is there anything between you and God? Or between you and another person? If so, clear up the rubble. Repent of it. The longer you hold on to the sin, the stronger its hold on you. God longs to set you free. He desires confession so that He can release His power in your life. Your communion with your heavenly Father is worth the effort to rid yourself of rubble. Victory is yours through Jesus Christ's blood. He is waiting for you to come with a repentant heart so that you can experience the fullness of His forgiveness and His love. Don't delay.

> *Dear forgiving Father, please keep me sensitive to the Holy Spirit's conviction of sin. May I not try to hide it or justify it. May I be quick to confess and repent, believing that Jesus' blood cleanses me from all sin. Help me to forgive just as You have forgiven me. Make me a clean vessel to hear the requests that You want to place on my heart. May I be one that You can count on to pray what is on Your heart. Give me a humble heart that cries out, "Search me, O God, and see if there be any wicked way in me." Oh, Father, may I clean up all the rubble so I can glorify You. In Jesus' name, amen.*

6. Thanksgiving: The Expression of a Grateful Heart

When my son Troy was about three years old, he loved to say the blessing at dinnertime. He would get out of his chair, walk around the table, point to the items, and pray, "God, thank You for the potatoes, thank You for the beans, thank You for the milk, thank You for . . ." We all waited until he completed his thanksgiving to the Lord before we began to eat the lukewarm food.

God had placed on Troy's young heart the importance of being thankful. As Scripture says, "Give thanks in all circumstances, for this is God's will for you in Christ Jesus" (1 Thessalonians 5:18). From Troy's perspective, God had provided food for a little boy's hungry tummy.

Giving thanks is the third step in our "Four Steps of Prayer." We establish a natural flow as we move from praise to confession because after we've worshiped our holy God, we want to be sure we are righteous in His eyes. Then, after confession, we feel thankful for God's mercy, which He extends to us in forgiving our sin.

During the thanksgiving time, we express our joy and gratitude for all God has done for us. Remember that praise focuses on *who* God is and thanksgiving on *what* God has done. Theologian O. Hallesby in his book *Prayer* says it this way, "When we give thanks we give God the glory for what He has done for us; and when we worship or give praise, we give God glory for what He is in Himself."[1]

Jesus expressed the importance of having a thankful heart in the story of the ten lepers in Luke 17. The lepers recognized Jesus and cried out to Him, "Jesus, Master, have pity on us!"

Can you hear the desperation in their voices? They were outcasts, ostracized from family and friends, suffering from a disease that was claiming their limbs and eventually their lives. Can you imagine the humiliation of having to cry out, "Unclean, unclean," so no one would come near?

Jesus heard their pleas and responded, "Go, show yourselves to the priests."

As the men went, their leprosy disappeared. What? Disappeared? No trace of the debilitating disease? They were healed. Now, wouldn't you think they would run to Jesus, throw their arms around Him and thank Him over and over?

But only one of them went back to Jesus. This former leper fell face down on the ground at Jesus' feet, thanking Him, for what He had done.

Jesus noticed. "Were not all ten cleansed? Where are the other nine?"

I pray that we are careful not to be like the nine. May we never take for granted God's gracious answer to our prayers, big or little.

Every week in Moms In Touch, thanksgiving is a set-aside, treasured time in which we express thanks to the Lord for His goodness in answering our prayers. Some weeks we marvel at how many prayers were answered. Many times God responded the very week we prayed; sometimes we waited months to see the answer, and sometimes years. At times we cried tears of joy, thanking God for answering a particular request.

One such time was when a group had prayed for a hard-hearted school principal. A mom reported, "God's reply was swift and surprising. He removed the man mid-term. A part-time principal was brought in, and we discovered he was a Christian. He was delighted by our prayer efforts on behalf of the school. My heart is smiling as I think of the way the Lord answered us. What a privilege to unite with the other moms and to offer our thanks to the One who answered immeasurably more than what we could imagine."

One group prayed for several weeks, asking God to protect every child at their elementary school. As one woman told the story, "One day parents, grandparents, and friends were lined up at the school's entrance to pick up their children. A grandmother's car went out of control, and she was unable to stop it. It careened onto the sidewalk and crashed through a wall of a kindergarten room. While the building was damaged, we thanked God for the way He answered our prayers of protection. Neither the grandmother nor any of the children were hurt."

Sharon admits, "Having a thankful heart is an ongoing challenge in the 'school' of my prayer life. However, 'practicing' thanksgiving each week in my prayer group for the past thirteen years has been like a weekly tutoring session."

I've found it helpful to keep a journal of answered prayer. Taking the time to write down the answers helps me to keep track of how God dealt with those for whom I've prayed. He wants us to remember His faithfulness—and to be thankful.

Rocks of Remembrance

When the children of Israel crossed the Jordan River, God taught them that remembering is an important part of thanksgiving.

> Now the Jordan is at flood stage all during harvest. Yet as soon as the priests who carried the ark reached the Jordan and their feet touched the water's edge, the water from upstream stopped flowing.... The priests who carried the ark of the covenant of the LORD stood firm on dry ground in the middle of the Jordan, while all Israel passed by.... When the whole nation had finished crossing the Jordan, the LORD said to Joshua, "Choose twelve men from among the people, one from each tribe, and tell them to take up twelve stones from the middle of the Jordan from right where the priests stood and to carry them over with you and put them down at the place where you stay tonight."
> (Joshua 3:15–4:3)

Why did God want them to make the stone altar?

In the future, when your descendants ask . . . , "What do these stones mean?" tell them, "Israel crossed the Jordan on dry ground." For the LORD your God dried up the Jordan before you until you had crossed over. . . . He did this so that all the peoples of the earth might know that the hand of the LORD is powerful and so that you might always fear the LORD your God. (Joshua 4:21–24)

What a privilege for us to pass down to our children and grand-children our "rocks of remembrance." Journaling will help us to do that, as we record answers to prayer.

Sometimes I'll pull down from the shelf my old prayer journals, and while I'm reading the answers to prayer, I'll become thankful all over again. In those times when we aren't seeing answers to our prayers, we can find comfort and encouragement as we go back to our journals and rehearse all the previous answers to prayer. I love that even in heaven there is a "scroll of remembrance . . . written in his presence concerning those who feared the LORD and honored his name" (Malachi 3:16).

Thankful in Season and Out

We are not only to thank God when our prayers are answered, when skies are blue and life is in the pink, but also when we don't see the answers to our prayers. Why? Because God is good.

The psalmist exclaims, "Give thanks to the LORD, for he is good; his love endures forever" (Psalm 136:1). God's goodness is from ever-lasting to everlasting. Yesterday He was good, today He is good, and tomorrow He will be good. A day will never come when He says, "Boy, you know, I feel cranky today. No one better cross me, or they're going to get it!" Everything He says is good, and everything He does is good. If we really believe that, thankfulness will flow no matter what happens—good or bad.

Are you healthy? God is good.
Do you have an illness? God is good.

Are you single? God is good.

Are you married? God is good.

Are you secure financially? God is good.

Are you in financial difficulty? God is good.

Are all your family members living? God is good.

Have you lost family members? God is good.

Do you have children? God is good.

Are you unable to have children? God is good.

Thanking God for His goodness in everything brings Him honor. Psalm 50:23 says, "He who sacrifices thank offerings honors me."

Sometimes it's hard to give thanks. My friend lost her husband suddenly, without time to say a proper good-bye. She also was facing financial difficulties, forcing her not only to deal with the emotions of losing her mate but also the added trauma of possibly losing her home. In the midst of her pain and sorrow, she gave thanks, even though she didn't understand why she had to suffer these losses. She believed Romans 8:28, that God was working all this together for good because He loved her. Her loving heavenly Father's promise gave her the courage and faith she needed.

> *Giving thanks doesn't have to originate with our feelings.*

Giving thanks doesn't have to originate with our feelings. Instead, by faith, we choose to thank God. That's what He has commanded us to do. And God never gives a command that isn't for our benefit, and He never will give us a command that He doesn't provide the strength and power to accomplish. When we choose to give thanks, we are giving a beautiful expression of confidence in God's perfect plan. And it's always a choice we're faced with—will we give thanks for this incident, or won't we?

I was running late one day and had an important meeting to attend. I always try to be punctual; being late is a big pet peeve. I dashed out the door, climbed into the car, put the key in the ignition, started the engine, and noticed the gas gauge was—yes, empty. My mind pictured the last person who used the car—and it wasn't me.

Was I going to give thanks? I wish I had because destruction was in the wake of my response. I stormed over to the offender and let him know how I felt. Did it fill up the gas tank? Did it make me feel better? No, it severed my relationship with him, with God, and with my emotional well-being.

Then there was the piano incident. When Rle and I were first married, God blessed us with a furnished home that we rented. That meant we could afford to buy a piano. As we moved over the years, this piano sat in several different living rooms, and it endured the wear and tear of children, friends, and piano lessons.

By the time our children became adults, I was pretty amazed that the piano was still in great shape. Then, one day as I was dusting, I noticed a water glass sitting on the piano's beautiful finished wood. My heart sank. Sure enough, I lifted the glass and saw the water stain.

This time I responded with thanks. I released *my* piano to the One who really owned it. And I covered up the water spot with a family picture.

The Benefits of Giving Thanks

I've learned that one of the benefits of giving thanks is experiencing God's rest. We can trust His heart even though we don't understand. In his book *Power in Praise,* Merlin Carothers states,

> There is nothing—no circumstance, no trouble, no testing— that can ever touch me until, first of all it has gone past God and past Christ, right through to me. If it has come that far, it has come with a great purpose, which I may not understand at the moment. But as I refuse to become panicky, as I lift up my eyes to Him and accept it as coming from the throne of God for some great purpose of blessing to my own heart, no sorrow will ever disturb me, no trial will ever disarm me, no circumstance will cause me to fret—for I shall rest in the joy of what my Lord is! That is the rest of victory.[2]

Another benefit of giving thanks is that your attitude changes. Thanksgiving crowds out depression, cynicism, fear, self-pity, and self-debasement. You begin to see the situation from a different perspective—from God's. It brings the light of God's presence into the situation.

My coauthor's husband became gravely ill as we worked together on this book. Loch was in the hospital for fifty days and had four surgeries, three of them in the span of eleven days. A couple of times, he almost died. Yet because Janet maintained an attitude of gratitude, she found reasons to be thankful rather than depressed or filled with self-pity each difficult day. Sometimes a nurse would walk by Loch's room and glance in to find him suffering from a bout of pain that was so great he couldn't ring the nurse's bell. Or a doctor would think of another way to approach the medical difficulties, and a breakthrough would occur.

> *Thanksgiving crowds out depression, cynicism, fear, self-pity, and self-debasement. You begin to see the situation from a different perspective— from God's.*

One day Loch's brother, who is a microbiologist, suggested that an infection specialist be called in to deal with a life-threatening infection that had the surgeons and internists stymied. Only one such specialist existed in the entire county, but a spot suddenly cleared in her schedule so she could take on Loch's case—and probably save his life.

Yes, the situation was dire, and Janet was pressed against the wall physically, emotionally, and spiritually. But because she gave thanks, she was able to see God at work daily, to know that He was present and that He cared.

Reeling or Resting

What are the consequences if we don't give thanks? Frustration! We can choose to continue our frustrated work or rest in God's finished work. God's desire is to conform us to His Son's image, changing us from glory to glory, making us more like Christ.

When life challenges you, threatening your family or your well-being, can you find it within yourself to give thanks? Or do you become so caught up in the circumstance that you aren't free to turn to God, thanking Him for His amazing ability to work on our behalf, both in the world and within our hearts?

I love how Ron Mehl in his book *God Works the Night Shift* says that all things *do* work together for good (Romans 8:28) as long as you know what that work is for. Romans 8:29 contains the answer: "For those God foreknew he also predestined to be conformed to the likeness of his Son, that he might be the firstborn among many brothers." Mehl says, "He is bending His power and His will to one purpose, and that is conforming you and me, His adopted children, to the image of the Lord Jesus. . . . If you know that He's going to use this or that or whatever to make you like the Savior, then you may take comfort in the fact that nothing in your life is wasted—no effort, no pain, no anxious moments, no tears are ever lost in some cosmic landfill."[3]

Another consequence of an unthankful spirit is that our prayers are hindered. A grumbling spirit can't coincide with the Spirit of Christ. Sometimes I think it's easier to give thanks for the catastrophic things than for the mundane duties of life.

How could I keep God's perspective when I made eight to ten sandwiches every day, plus all the other edibles I was putting in those brown bags? Some mornings, when my children were growing up, I simply didn't want to make all those lunches.

I confess I didn't *feel* thankful, but as an act of obedience, I decided to practice the principle of giving thanks. Something happened to my spirit when I started to give thanks. I thanked God I was physically able to do it, that I had children to do it for, and that we could provide healthy lunches. As I gave thanks, the Holy Spirit brought to mind that I could pray for each of my children as I made their lunches. I asked God that as they ate their meal they would know how much I loved them and that they would know that we don't live by bread alone but by every word that proceeds out of God's mouth. I was amazed at the thoughts God gave me to pray as I went about the mundane task of preparing lunches. I was doing something that the world might see as insignificant, but in light of eternity, I was making a difference in my children's lives.

Through the power of prayer—the simple act of giving thanks—God transformed a mundane task into an act of eternal significance. He can do the same in your life.

Marika, a mom in Jerusalem, walked with Amir, her seventeen-year-old son, to his school every Tuesday morning so she could join other moms to pray for the school. The first prayer meeting after the summer break was scheduled for a bright morning. As Marika and her son walked, they were engrossed in conversation about his future when "we both jumped because of an enormous bang!" she recounted. "We stared, speechless, at the precise spot we had passed only forty seconds before, the spot where a bomb exploded."

Amir, in shock, could only stare seemingly without seeing. Marika burst into tears. "Tears of anger and frustration over who could do such a thing, over what could have happened to us, but also tears of awe over what had not happened to us," she said.

The two made their way through the smoke, confusion, and array of wrecked cars. People were wailing, sirens were blaring. This mom and her son found themselves sitting on the steps of the school. As Marika hugged her son, she realized that his future, which they had been discussing with such intensity, almost had been shattered. "We both thanked the Lord for His protection and also prayed for strength for the day."

Later, the moms met for prayer. They had a very different agenda that day than they thought they would. They prayed for the wounded and for the family of the suicide bomber.

"Every morning," Marika said, "already for years, we pray that the Lord will watch our going out and coming in. God is our refuge and strength. Amir was in shock for several days, but he eventually came back to the world. We are thankful."

When we choose to give thanks even though the circumstances are less than wonderful, 2 Chronicles says that the glory of the Lord will fill the temple (7:1). We are the Holy Spirit's temple, and when we give thanks, the Lord's glory is seen—in us.

And, you know, an unthankful spirit might catch up with us when we least expect it. A mother had invited some people for dinner, and as everyone was seated around the table, the mom suggested her little girl ask the blessing. The little girl responded, "Oh, but I wouldn't know what to say." The mother replied, "Just say what you hear Mommy say." The little girl bowed her head. "Dear God, why on earth did I invite all these people to dinner?"

Doesn't it make you wonder what the mother's body language was as she prepared the meal? What did she say while she worked that her little girl overheard? Knowing that little ears are around can be a wonderful—or frightening—accountability.

I agree with my friend Pam when she contends, "I believe that my faith becomes more 'perfected' as I choose to give thanks and acknowledge that to give thanks comes not as a request but a command to obey—'Give thanks in all circumstances, for this is God's will for you in Christ Jesus'" (1 Thessalonians 5:18).

Let's Pray

Prayers of thanksgiving are expressions of appreciation and gratefulness for God's answers. During this time, don't ask for anything; only offer your thanksgiving. Remember, praise focuses on *who* God is and thanksgiving on *what* God has done.

Meditate on these questions and write down your thanksgiving:

What were the circumstances of your salvation? Thank God for every detail He put in place that caused you to come to Him.

In what ways have you felt God's love? Thank Him.

Think back over the past week or month. How has God shown His faithfulness to you (providing help, strength, wisdom)? Give thanks.

What trial are you going through? Thank Him and experience His rest.

Giving Thanks *In* vs. *For*

But, you might say, if we're to give thanks in all things, doesn't that mean we thank God for evil? I think the key word here is "in," not "for." The Lord tells us to give thanks "in" all things not "for" all things. We aren't thankful for the evil—the murders, rapes, sickness, disease, and divorce. God is greater than the sin or the circumstance. He can override the evil and bring victory to the situation.

Giving thanks helps me to surrender to God. We're never to let circumstances dampen our thanksgiving, for He is greater than any situation.

What about those unexpected interruptions that can so easily irritate us? We somehow forget that at the beginning of the day we prayed, "Dear Father, I give You this day. I yield myself to You." Then we make our plans for the day, and sure enough, our plans are interrupted. What do we do with the interruption?

I remember one such day when it seemed I was never going to get to my "to-do" list. As my children were leaving for school, Trisha, who was in middle school at the time, complained of an earache. I thought, *I really don't have time for an earache today of all days. This definitely is not on my to-do list!*

The practice of giving thanks came to the surface, and my anxiety about accomplishing things faded away. "Okay, Lord, You know all the things on my platter for today. I don't know how I'm going to get everything done, but I'm going to give You thanks for this interruption in 'my' schedule." As peace settled in my heart, I tended to a sick little girl who needed a mother's comfort and love, making sure she felt she was my most important priority. She certainly didn't need a mom that made her feel guilty and as if she were a nuisance.

I will never forget the sweet time I had with Trisha that day. I can still see in my mind's eye the two of us in the waiting room at the doctor's office, her head lying in my lap as I stroked her hair, silently praying for her. Jesus was there.

When we are obedient to give thanks, the Lord will send something sweet and precious our way that wasn't on our to-do list.

I remember a wise mother, Jane, sharing with me the story of her son's coming to her after a few months of marriage. He began to complain to her about the things that were bugging him about his new bride, Sandra. After he expressed his criticisms, Jane shared with her son everything she was thankful for concerning Sandra. Jane brought up specific incidents and character qualities that she loved about Sandra and how grateful Jane was that this woman was his wife. A few months passed, and the son mentioned that his mom's response about Sandra showed him what his mom really thought of his wife. Jane's thankful heart toward Sandra reminded him of the reasons he had married her. He went home thankful to God for the wife the Lord had given him.

When we are intentional about being thankful, it produces in us a gracious spirit. I love the movie *Gone With the Wind*. Melanie is my favorite character. She saw the best in Scarlett, even though Scarlett was cunning, deceitful, self-serving, and vicious. Melanie was always kind and loving.

I have a friend, Judy, who lives in Canada, who is like Melanie. I've actually told her I thought she was an angel unaware. I don't think I've ever heard her say a cruel word about anyone. The spirit of thankfulness in all things makes Judy beautiful. She is filled with the Holy Spirit. Paul says, "Be filled with the Spirit ... giving thanks always for all things unto God" (Ephesians 5:18, 20 KJV). It goes hand in hand. The fruit of the Spirit is love, joy, peace, patience, kindness, goodness, faithfulness, gentleness, and self-control. The fragrance of a thankful life splashes Jesus onto everyone we meet. A person who chooses to give thanks isn't a grumbler or a complainer; she is a "thanker."

I want to be a person who recognizes that every good gift comes from God, and to always write Him a thank-you note in the form of a prayer. How about you?

> *Dear sovereign Lord, please help me to express my thanks to You through prayer. May I never neglect being grateful for Your bountiful provision. Help me to turn to You in thanks even when I face trials and suffering. I ask that my trust would be in the character of who You are, believing that all these things will work together for good, and that You know perfectly how to conform me to the image of Your Son. Lord, teach me to give thanks in all things. In Jesus' name, amen.*

7. Intercession:
Standing in the Gap

"Looking at the words scrawled across my computer screen, I felt numb with disbelief," Susan recounted to me. "A threat had been made against our high school. According to the email, which was distributed by our principal, a teacher had found a message written on a desk warning that on the following Tuesday, 'Westmont High School will die.'"

At first Susan was stunned. Violence in schools happened in far-away places, affecting children and teachers whose names she didn't know. But this threat was directed at the school where *her* children attended and would, according to the note, be carried out in only four days.

"The principal's message," Susan continued, "informed us that extra security measures would be taken, including the addition of plainclothes police officers on campus the following week." The night before the possible attack, concerned Christian parents implemented their own security measures, praying together for the would-be perpetrator to be caught. "We lifted our children and our school before the Lord and asked God to confuse Satan's plans," Susan said.

On Tuesday morning the parents learned that the student who had made the threat had been found and arrested Monday night—at the very time the group had been praying.

What if Susan and the others hadn't interceded on behalf of the school that night? What if they hadn't taken a prayerful stand against the Devil's schemes?

These Christians were ready to pray. They were ready for the fourth step in the prayer sequence: intercession. Before they interceded, they took time to worship, to focus on their almighty, sovereign, and faithful God. They praised Him for who He is. Then they confessed, which brought them to a humble position, seeking God to reveal to them any sin that would block their confidence in asking during the intercession. Joyfully they gave thanks for how God had answered prayer increasing their faith. At that point, their hearts were prepared to ask in believing prayer for the safety of their school and the children. God responded.

Who is an intercessor? Simply someone who prays for another, one who pleads before God's throne on behalf of another.

Abraham was a fervent intercessor. He interceded on behalf of his nephew Lot, pleading that God would save the righteous (including his nephew) in Sodom and Gomorrah. Abraham asked God to withhold His destruction of the city if fifty righteous people resided there. God answered Abraham and said He wouldn't destroy the city if fifty righteous people could be found there. Abraham's bold intercession continued as he asked the Lord not to destroy the city if forty-five righteous people were located. God complied. Then Abraham asked for forty, then thirty, then twenty, and then ten. Each time God answered Abraham's request with a yes. But as we know, not even ten righteous people lived in the city. Still, God saved Lot and his family (Genesis 18–19).

What a beautiful picture Abraham, the intercessor, gives us of going before God to obtain mercy for someone in need. When we come to our almighty, omnipotent God in prayer for others, God hears and answers our prayers, if we pray according to His Word and His will. God has given us the responsibility to stand in the gap for others. The phrase "stand in the gap" appears in Ezekiel 22:30, "And I sought for a man among them, that should make up the hedge, and stand in the gap before me for the land, that I should not destroy it;

but I found none" (KJV). What a sobering verse. God is speaking, and He is saying He would have saved the entire nation of Israel if just one person had cried for mercy on the nation's behalf. One voice could have brought God's deliverance. James 4:2 comes to life in that context when it says that we have not because we ask not.

Author F. B. Meyers writes, "The great tragedy of life is not unanswered prayer but unoffered prayer."

Interceding with Authority

An intercessor is not only one who stands in the gap but is also one who takes seriously her authority (her position) in Christ. She prays with confidence because she knows she has been made worthy by Jesus' blood, and she knows that praying in His name will pierce the darkness and cause the stronghold to tumble down. She remembers who she is and is secure in her identity—redeemed, saved by grace, and dutifully standing between the need and her almighty God.

In the book *Beyond the Veil*, Alice Smith describes it this way: "The word *intercede* is like the word 'intercept'; to intercept something you must stop or interrupt its progress or course of action. The intercessor intercepts the plans of the enemy and causes a spiritual interchange ... meaning to replace one thing with another."[1]

That's what happened when the parents prayed against the Devil's schemes for their threatened school. God calls on us to participate through prayer in the fulfillment of His divine plans—not our plans. The Holy Spirit will lay on our hearts the things that are on God's heart. When we ask according to His will, it will be done. We can expect the answer because our prayer is accomplishing God's purpose.

When we rest in the truth that it's all about God and not about us, our prayers take on a freshness, and praying isn't so laborious. Sometimes we get tired because we're working so hard to convince God instead of relaxing in His will. When Jesus said, "Ask, and it will be given to you" (Matthew 7:7), He was telling us to bring our need before the Father, leave it there, and trust that in His holy plan it would be answered perfectly. We don't have to coerce, beg, or present reasons we think the request should be answered a particular way. That's exhausting mentally, physically, and spiritually. We can just leave the need, the burden, the concern with the One who says that when we ask, the tide of battle turns. Yes, even when we can't see it.

Jennifer Kennedy Dean states it this way:

> To ask is simply to take the need—not the answer—to the Father. "They have no more wine" (Jn. 2:3). "The one you love is sick" (Jn. 11:3). "Your will be done on earth as it is in heaven" (Mt. 6:10). "Father, glorify your name" (Jn. 12:28). When you realize how sweetly uncomplicated presenting your petitions to your Father is, then your energies can be devoted to worshiping Him, loving Him, hearing Him, and letting Him recreate the inner landscape of your soul.[2]

Our part in intercessory prayer is to pray in the Spirit (Ephesians 6:18). Praying in the Spirit means that Jesus is in control of our lives and self is not in control. With all known sin confessed, the Holy Spirit places on our hearts the prayers that are from the Father's heart. We are praying as Jesus would pray. As we pray according to the Holy Spirit's prompting, we experience His peace.

> *When we rest in the truth that it's all about God and not about us, our prayers take on a freshness, and praying isn't so laborious.*

Author Dick Eastman states that there is no higher calling than that of an intercessor. "It is God's method for involving His followers more completely in the totality of His plan. In no other way can the believer become as fully involved with God's work . . . as in intercessory prayer."[3] We can have no greater ministry, no greater work than to pray for others.

Andrew Murray, in his book *Prayer: A 31-Day Plan to Enrich Your Prayer Life* says,

> God rules the world and His Church through the prayers of His people. That God should have made the extension of His kingdom to such a large extent dependent on the faithfulness of His

people in prayer is a stupendous mystery and yet an absolute certainty. God calls for intercessors: in His grace He has made His work dependent on them; He waits for them. . . . The power of heaven was to be at their disposal. The grace and power of God waited for man's bidding.[4]

We can stand in the gap for a wayward son or daughter, between your child and a bullying child, for your school as it considers a humanistic curriculum, for children addicted to drugs and alcohol, for young people who are engaging in premarital sex, and for a child who is abused mentally, emotionally, physically, or spiritually.

Being a "Mat Carrier"

The joy of praying with others is having intercessors join you. I love the idea of moms being "mat carriers" for one another's children. In Mark 2, Jesus was teaching and healing in a family's "living room."

> So many gathered that there was no room left, not even outside the door. . . . Some men came, bringing to him a paralytic, carried by four of them. Since they could not get him to Jesus because of the crowd, they made an opening in the roof above Jesus and, after digging through it, lowered the mat the paralyzed man was lying on. When Jesus saw their faith, he said to the paralytic, "Son, your sins are forgiven. . . . But that you may know that the Son of Man has authority on earth to forgive sins . . . I tell you, get up, take your mat and go home."

Four men took their sick friend to Jesus. They just knew that if they could get to Him, Jesus would heal him. They took time from their busy lives to each grab a corner of the mat, pick up their friend, and walk for who-knows-how-far.

Even a crowd didn't deter them. They had the audacity to climb to the top of another man's house and dig a hole in his roof so they could lower their paralyzed friend in front of Jesus. These men took an impossible situation and brought it face-to-face with Jesus, who made the impossible possible. Can you imagine the four men peering down through the hole in the roof anticipating a miracle? Then Jesus looks up at them and tells them that because of their faith He would heal their friend. The men's faith, not the sick fellow's faith, brought about the miracle.

Intercessors are like those four men. They each take a corner of the mat and lower their loved ones, one at a time, to Jesus. Many of our children are paralyzed by sin, and the weight of that reality is too much for a parent to bear by herself. We become weary when we don't see any change, when we don't spy even a glimpse of an answer to prayer.

Imagine a mom pulling one corner of a mat, as she slowly drags her two-hundred-pound football player of a son to Jesus. But then another mom comes alongside and picks up a corner. The prayers of the second mom spark faith. Then another mom and another come alongside, each gathering up a corner. Hope returns, as she hears the believing prayers of the other moms.

After going through a frustrating, exhausting time with one of her children, Jodie found the burden overwhelming. So she went to her prayer group and admitted what was happening in her family. "I dished out the sordid details of my story," she said, "and found my family and myself the recipients of some of the most incredible, faith-filled, powerful prayers I've ever heard."

How blessed we can be to have other moms faithfully help us to carry our mat, like the ailing man whose friends carried his mat to bring him to Jesus. It doesn't matter that some of the children are rebellious, indifferent, or dead in their faith. They have no defense against us putting them on the mat. Jesus looks at the hopeful, prayerful faces of the mat-carriers and says, "Son, your sins are forgiven" (Mark 2:5).

One of the greatest joys for an intercessor is to pray for the salvation of others. Placing each person on the mat and pouring out intercessions is a beautiful privilege. We can pray that our loved ones' hearts would be receptive (Luke 8:8, 15), that their spiritual eyes would be open (2 Corinthians 4:3–4), that they would be delivered from the power and persuasions of the Evil One (2 Corinthians 10:3–4), and that they would repent and accept Christ (2 Corinthians 7:10).

Throughout Trisha's high school years we prayed for the salvation of two of her "guy friends." She invited them to an evangelistic crusade and, not having her license yet, asked if I would drive. Of course, I was delighted to take her and her friends. During the message, one of the boys was squirming and humming to himself. I thought, *How on earth is this young man going to accept Christ? He's not even listening.* But when the invitation was given, both boys asked Trisha to go down on the field with them to accept Christ. God had heard our prayers and had softened the soil of each young man's heart. That memorable night, they were both delivered from the Evil One's power and persuasions. The angels were dancing, and so were Trisha and I.

When we intercede for one another's children on a regular basis a sincere love for them develops. You become an extended prayer family, caring greatly for each other's children and seeing them as your own.

As an intercessor, you can leave a lasting legacy of prayer. What a joy to pray for each one of your children, their spouses or spouses-to-be, their children, and *their* spouses that they would love the Lord with all their heart and be devoted to Him. What a thrill to know that long after we've passed away, our children and great-great-grandchildren will live in the atmosphere of our prayers.

Praying for generations to come is biblical. One day as I was reading Jesus' famous prayer in John 17, the truth of verse 20 grabbed my heart. Jesus says, "My prayer is not for them alone. I pray also for those who will believe in me through their message, that all of them may be one, Father, just as you are in me and I am in you." He was praying for you and for me at that very moment. And now we are basking in Jesus' prayer-covering two thousand years later.

On realizing this startling truth, I read the whole chapter and was touched by the intercessory requests that He prayed to the Father for me: that the Father would protect me by the power of His name; that I would be one in Them as They were one; that I would be protected from the Evil One; that I would have the full measure of Jesus' joy; that I would be sanctified by the truth of the Word of God and so much more.

I took these same requests that Jesus prayed for me and I prayed them for my children and their children. And I've witnessed some of the answers. All four of my children have chosen godly mates, and my little grandson, Joshua, has a praying mom and dad who are teaching him the ways of the Lord. I might not know Joshua's children, but my prayers for them are just as valid.

Amy Carmichael's statement inspires and motivates me. "We have such few years to gain the victory and all of eternity to enjoy them."

Praying Scripture

So an intercessor is one who stands in the gap, one who carries the mat for a needy friend. And an intercessor uses Scripture as one of the most important weapons in praying for others. An intercessor prays back to God His very words on behalf of the one for whom she is interceding.

Satan's attacks can be thwarted by the power of God's living Word. Jeremiah speaks of this when he declares, "'Is not my word like fire?' declares the LORD, 'like a hammer that breaks a rock in pieces?'" (Jeremiah 23:29). The Word is like a hammer that convicts, crushes the hardness that encases hearts, and brings to repentance a stiff-necked, egocentric person.

Jesus Himself used the Scripture to defeat Satan while being tempted in the wilderness. "It has been written, man shall not live and be upheld and sustained by bread alone, but by every word that comes forth from the mouth of God" (Matthew 4:4, AMP).

God's Word also teaches us how to pray rightly. When we pray back Scripture, we're praying God's will. This brings peace, faith, and hope to an anxious heart because God's Word says, "My word that goes forth out of My mouth, it shall not return to Me void—without producing any effect, useless—but it shall accomplish that which I please and purpose, and it shall prosper in the thing for which I sent it" (Isaiah 55:11, AMP).

One mom wrote how using Scripture in prayer had transformed her. "I learned how to walk consistently and to lean on God's Word for guidance and direction in my life and my children's lives. The whole experience has changed me from the inside-out by stirring up an intense yearning to know and apply His Word to my life."

Barbara, a prayer group leader for Hendersonville High School, tells of an unusual prayer her group prayed for the students: "I shall not die, but live to tell of all His deeds" (Psalm 118:17, TLB). In the previous school year several students had died; so the moms faithfully prayed for protection, using the verse from the Psalms as their base.

"Every Thursday, we prayed through the yearbook alphabetically, praying for twenty different students each week," Barbara explained. "On November 9 we prayed for a group that included Josh, one of my son's best friends. Two days later Josh was in a terrible car accident. He was driving home with his friend, Kiara. Going too fast, he ran off the road, and his car rolled over four times. When the police saw the pancake-like vehicle, they couldn't believe the kids survived. And without a scratch! Kiara's seatbelt failed to hold her; so she ended up in the backseat. The roof over her front seat had been crushed so badly she wouldn't have survived. And somehow the roof above Josh stopped just short of his head. Another friend, an exchange student from Albania who never wears a seatbelt, was supposed to have been in the backseat. He had decided not to ride in the car at the last minute. The car barely missed a huge tree but was stopped by a mailbox that had been put in the week before. I told Josh, 'The message is this: God hears our prayers—every one!' Prayer is power, power over Satan's plans, power that is God-given."

Irene knew the power of praying Scripture and regularly placed her child's name into verses. One week she prayed 1 John 2:16 for her daughter, "For everything in the world—the cravings of sinful man, the lust of his eyes and the boasting of what he has and does—comes not from the Father but from the world." As Irene prayed this Scripture for her daughter, the phrase "the lust of eyes" kept coming to her mind. Many times throughout the day, Irene prayed that the Lord would protect Jody from anything that her eyes shouldn't see.

That week Jody, who was in the fifth grade, was invited by a friend to spend the night with her and two other friends. During the course of the evening, the friend went into her brother's bedroom to pull out a magazine and then lured the girls into the bathroom. She proceeded to open a pornographic magazine. Jody said, "It's not right; I'm leaving." As she left, one of the other girls followed her.

Irene didn't find out until weeks later what had happened. The girl that left with Jody told her mom about the incident and said how glad she was that Jody said something. It gave her the courage to also do what was right.

Jody was tested, but through the power of God's Word uttered in prayer, she withstood the test. And Irene's faith increased as she saw her prayers answered.

Probably one of the Scriptures moms pray most often is the one Jesus prayed for the disciples and for us in John 17:15, "Protect them from the evil one." To stand in the gap between our children and Satan through praying the Word is powerful. I have no idea how many times my children were saved from life-destroying decisions, from evil people, or from circumstances because of praying that Scripture.

When I pray Zechariah 2:5, "Father, I ask that you will be a wall of fire around them, and the glory within," I think of God Almighty as that fire around them, burning up anything that comes close to harm them. What a wonderful picture of God's protection.

Not only do I pray for God to protect my loved ones from evil, but I also pray that God would keep them from doing evil. I ask Him to strengthen their inner man to resist Satan's temptations. I use the Scripture Jesus prayed for Peter when Satan asked Jesus if he could come against Peter. Jesus said to Peter, "Simon, Simon, Satan has asked to sift you as wheat. But I have prayed for you, Simon, that your faith may not fail" (Luke 22:31).

One day during Trisha's senior year in college, she called spiritually weary. Over a period of time her unsaved friends had hurled many questions at her about her faith. Some of the questions were thought provoking and seemingly unanswerable. She felt confused and battle weary as over and over she graciously defended her faith. Trisha had tried to live out 1 Peter 3:15, "But in your hearts set apart Christ as Lord. Always be prepared to give an answer to everyone who asks you to give the reason for the hope that you have. But do this with gentleness and respect."

Her friends' heady questions had brought about some questioning of her own. Now, in my earlier prayer years, I would have prayed, "Lord, keep these questioning friends away from Trisha. They are weakening her faith." Instead, I realized I needed to pray that her faith would not fail. It was a time to pray for her to be strengthened in her inner being. Going through this caused Trisha to become more diligent in reading the Bible, seeking godly counsel, and reading books on how to defend her faith.

Praying Specifically

Another important way for an intercessor to pray besides praying Scripture is to pray specifically. Matthew 20:29–34 tells the story of two blind men. They were sitting by the side of the road when they heard that Jesus was going by. They began to shout, "Lord, Son of David, have mercy on us!" The crowd wanted them to be quiet, but they shouted all the louder. Let's pick up the story in verse 32. "Jesus stopped and called them. 'What do you want me to do for you?' he asked. 'Lord,' they answered, 'we want our sight.' Jesus had compassion on them and touched their eyes. Immediately they received their sight and followed him."

Now Jesus knew all along what they needed, but He wanted them to verbalize their need, to say aloud what they wanted Him to do.

What is your need? What are your children's needs, your family's, your church's, your community's? Jesus is saying, "What do you want Me to do for you?"

Mrs. Cowman in the book *Streams in the Desert* encourages us to "make your requests with definite earnestness if you would have definite answers. Aimlessness in prayer accounts for so many seemingly unanswered prayers.... Fill out your check for something definite, and it will be cashed at the bank of Heaven when presented in Jesus' name. Dare to be definite with God."[5]

Let's Pray

As an intercessor, you have the privilege and responsibility to stand in the gap for others before God's throne of grace.

Pray back God's very words on behalf of the one for whom you are interceding. Ask boldly, believing the promises of God's Word. (Place the person's name in the blank space.) Other Scripture passages for a variety of circumstances can be found on pages 203–204. Also, on pages 198–199 is a list of topics you could pray for each day of the week since sometimes the needs of individuals and the world can overwhelm an intercessor.

Relationship with God. "Merciful Lord, I ask that _____ will love You with all his heart and with all his soul and with all his mind." (Matthew 22:37)

Trials, temptation, suffering. "Caring Father, thank You that You have redeemed _____ and summoned him by name. He is Yours. I rejoice in Your promise that when _____ passes through the waters, You are with him. When he passes through the rivers, they will not sweep over him. And when he walks through the fire, he will not be burned." (Isaiah 43:1–2)

Protection from the Evil One. "Almighty God, You are faithful. I pray that You would strengthen and protect _____ from the Evil One." (2 Thessalonians 3:3)

Obedience to parents. "Loving Father, please teach _____ that only fools refuse to be taught. May _____ listen to his father and mother, for what he learns from them will stand him in good stead; and it will gain him many honors. I ask that _____ will obey his father and his mother." (Proverbs 1:8–9; 6:20, TLB)

Growth in Christ. "Dear Lord, just as _____ received Christ Jesus as Lord, may _____ continue to live in him, rooted and built up in him, strengthened in the faith as _____ was taught, and overflowing with thankfulness." (Colossians 2:6)

Power in weakness. "Almighty God, may _____ experience Your grace that is sufficient for him, for Your power is made perfect in weakness. May _____ boast all the more gladly about his weaknesses, so that Christ's power may rest on him." (2 Corinthians 12:9)

Joyful, patient, and faithful. "Heavenly Father, develop in _____ these character qualities: joyful in hope, patient in affliction, faithful in prayer." (Romans 12:12)

Staying pure. "All-knowing God, I ask that _____ would flee from the evil desires of youth and pursue righteousness, faith, love, and peace, along with those who call on the Lord out of a pure heart." (2 Timothy 2:22)

Praying Boldly

An intercessor prays daring prayers. Jesus gives us a vivid picture of this kind of praying in Luke 11. A man has a friend come to visit and has nothing to feed him. So he goes to his neighbor at midnight banging at the door asking his friend for three loaves of bread. Now part of the audacity of this request is that one loaf of bread was a day's supply, and he asked for three. Sometimes we are afraid to ask God for too much. It just seems too big, too hard for God to do. What an insult to the King of Kings and Lord of Lords, Creator of heaven and earth, to imply that He can't do something. He is able. He is honored when we bring to Him large petitions.

Mr. Crandle had a reputation for being the toughest teacher at the elementary school. Many a fourth grader responded with fear and trembling upon learning their fifth-grade fate—a year in Mr. Crandle's room. One year a Moms In Touch group received a prayer request from the mother of a girl in Mr. Crandle's room. The sensitive fifth grader was scared to death of him. She couldn't handle yelling. She was struggling with all the homework. She was in tears every evening.

The concerns of this family were lifted before the Lord week after week as the group asked that Mr. Crandle would refrain from yelling.

Old habits are hard to break, and the moms knew only the Lord could give a man the wisdom to control his tongue.

Kathy, the MITI leader, was working in Mr. Crandle's classroom when he said to her, "I always start out the school year being really tough and doing a lot of yelling. It gets the kids' attention right off the bat, lets them know who's in charge. It just doesn't seem to be working with this class. I'm going to have to find a different tactic!"

He went on to share that a family had come to him whose little girl was terrified of him. Then he said, "I wouldn't want to damage one of these little ones entrusted to me for anything in the world." God truly works in response to prayer. Mr. Crandle found a new way to relate to his students.

Jesus' "work" is intercession, and so is ours. We are joining Him in this great work. First Timothy 2:1, 3–4 says, "I urge, then, first of all, that requests, prayers, intercession and thanksgiving be made for everyone.... This is good, and pleases God our Savior, who wants all men to be saved and to come to a knowledge of the truth." "Therefore, my dear [sister], stand firm. Let nothing move you. Always give yourselves fully to the work of the Lord, because you know that your labor in the Lord is not in vain" (1 Corinthians 15:58).

> *Almighty God, who is able to answer all our prayers, I ask that You would help me to be an intercessor that You can count on to pray the things on Your heart. Help me to believe beyond a shadow of a doubt that Satan's attack can be destroyed by the power of the living Word of God. I ask that I would not pray vaguely but make specific requests. May I pray bold and daring prayers on behalf of others. May I not tire of standing in the gap. I pray that You would pour out upon me a spirit of intercession. And may I expect to see Your goodness in the land of the living. Amen.*

Part 3

*Praying as Deep as Your Heart and
as Wide as Your World*

6. Praying According to God's Promises

As a child, in my Sunday school class we sang a little chorus,

Every promise in the book is mine,
Every chapter, every verse, every line.
All the blessings of His love Divine.
Every promise in the book is mine.

Is that an overstatement? Are all the promises really ours? When we pray, we need to pray with confidence. And that confidence is based on knowing for sure that the promise we claim is for us today.

When you pray, do you know which promises in Scripture are for us to claim today and which were for a specific people or a specific situation? The differentiation obviously is important to make.

Just because we pray a promise doesn't guarantee that the prayer will be answered as we expect. Cassandra knows that all too well. Here's how she tells her story:

"When our children were preschoolers, I met with a dear friend once a week to pray for our four kids. After that, not a year went by that I didn't lead a prayer group and have a faithful band of women praying for my children, as I prayed for theirs. We prayed God's promises for our kids, for them to exhibit godly character traits, and of course, for a godly life mate for each of them.

"From a young age our daughter, Melissa, exhibited a strong sense of God's call on her life. She accepted the Lord at an early age, and even in kindergarten she told her friends about Jesus. During elementary school she read through the Bible several times on her own and memorized large portions of Scripture. Her heart was drawn toward missions, and her goal was to go into some type of Christian service. She was one of those trouble-free kids, and we delighted in her walk with God.

"But sometime during her college years, the spiritual climate of Melissa's heart must have changed. Since we lived far from the college, we didn't detect the change. When she graduated from college, the unthinkable happened. She dated a young man from a different religious faith. Despite our expressed concerns, Melissa eventually married him.

"Over the years, God had answered so many prayers on our behalf, but He seemed unmoved by our requests that Melissa marry someone who shared her desire to serve the Lord. The choice of a godly life mate is such an important decision, affecting generations to come. As I reflected on her earlier passion for God, my heart broke.

"Then, as I read through Isaiah, I was struck with the anguish of God's heart over His wayward daughter, Israel. Every other page was 'wet with His tears,' the tears of a Father, exposing His broken heart.

"Finally the light dawned for me: How could I understand God's broken heart for His world, unless my heart was broken first? Through this I learned to pray from a broken heart for the prodigal world. I realized that what I labeled 'unanswered' prayer might truly be a path to knowing God in a more personal way. He might have deeper truths to teach me through my disappointments and unanswered prayers. While we still pray for Melissa and her husband, we now see the situation in a different light."

What is a promise? The *American Heritage Dictionary* says, "A declaration assuring that one will or will not do something." How disappointing when you have been promised something, and then the person reneges. Many times those broken promises can leave us with broken hearts.

But we need never fear that God will break our hearts by not keeping a promise He has made. He is a promise keeper. David says of God in Psalm 138:2, "For your promises are backed by all the honor of your name" (TLB).

Life can be painful. Sickness, death, accidents, and cataclysmic events can disrupt the flow of our lives, leaving us fearful. God will allow some storms in our lives to test us to trust Him and His Word. In Mark 4 we find the story of the disciples in the middle of a storm— a storm the Lord led them into. Jesus said, "Let us go over to the other side." Being omniscient (all knowing) He knew what was going to happen.

Picture in your mind the raging waters, the dark clouds, the violent waves lashing at the boat. The disciples' faces are filled with fear as they furiously work to stay afloat. They almost reach the point of exhaustion. These were professional fisherman; they had been in storms before, but no matter how hard they tried, they couldn't control this situation. And where was Jesus? Asleep in the back of the boat. How could He be asleep? Didn't He care? Didn't He notice they were hanging on for dear life?

After exhausting their own resources, they cried out in a panic to Jesus, "Teacher, don't You even care that we are all about to drown?"

Do you try to control your situations by using your own wisdom, strength, and resources? And then seeing that nothing has worked, do you desperately cry out to Jesus, "Lord, don't You see what is happening? I'm drowning!"

Jesus is in your boat! Whatever situation you are in, whatever trial you are going through, He's in your boat! He wants to reveal His power and display His glory. When we experience storms—and we will—God is saying to us, "Will you trust Me? Will you believe My promises? I implore you, Call unto me and I will answer you and show you great and mighty things you do not know. My ears are attentive to your cry. For I know the plans I have for you, and they are for good and not for evil, to give you a future and a hope. My grace is sufficient for you, for my power is made perfect in weakness"(Jeremiah 33:3; Psalm 34:15; Jeremiah 29:11; 2 Corinthians 12:9).

God longs for us to trust Him. He desires that believers mix His promises with faith. The way we respond to difficulties, to the storms, is related directly to how well we know God. We can trust someone we know. Rest comes in trusting His unfailing love for us and believing that He will never withhold anything from us that is in our best interest. That's why we can thank Him ahead of time that He will fulfill His promises even though we haven't tasted the answer.

Unfulfilled Promises?

But what about those times we feel we've prayed for something based on a promise in Scripture and God's answer doesn't begin to resemble what we had asked for?

Dr. De Haan offers insight.

Failure to understand a promise in its context can lead to some very bad conclusions. Too many people go around quoting Bible verses as promises to them as individuals when in fact the promises were given to specific biblical characters, a nation, or only to people of a certain time period.[1]

Even though some promises were given to specific people, can't the principles apply to us? De Haan answers yes and no.

If the promise reflects an unchanging characteristic of God and how He relates to us, then we can reasonably assume that because He is unchanging He will continue to reflect that promise in relating to other people. For example, when the Lord told the apostle Paul, "my strength is made perfect in weakness," He was addressing a specific situation in Paul's life—the "thorn in the flesh" of 2 Corinthians 12:7–10. Yet that truth applies to all people who recognize their weakness and reach out to God for strength." (Ephesians 1:19)[2]

An example of a promise that we can't claim is one given to Joshua when the Lord said, "I will give you every place where you set your foot"(Joshua 1:3). This verse doesn't mean that if you spy a great piece of land and walk around the perimeter in your Reeboks that the property will become yours. Yet some have used this verse to claim a troubled neighborhood back for God, as they have prayer-walked around the streets. Yes, it is God's will that He be supreme in our communities, but to claim this verse as a promise is a faulty assumption.

The *principle* found in the verse can be applied by praying, "Father, as we walk around this neighborhood, we ask that the ground that has been given over to Satan will once again be Yours." This certainly is God's will. We just need to be careful about claiming a promise that was given to a biblical person for a specific reason.

Unconditional and Conditional Promises

Some of God's promises are unconditional and some are conditional. What's an unconditional promise? De Haan states, "He promises to hold up His end of the agreement no matter what we do. . . . The fulfillment of unconditional promises does not depend on the faithfulness of people, but only on God. Even if we are unfaithful, God cannot be anything but faithful to His word (2 Timothy 2:13)."[3]

These are unconditional promises:

> God told Noah He would never again send a worldwide flood (Genesis 9:8–17).
> David received assurance that his royal line would last forever (2 Samuel 7:16).
> Jesus said He would return to earth to reward the righteous and punish the wicked (Matthew 16:27; 25:31–46).
> Jesus promised that after He ascended to heaven He would send the Holy Spirit (John 16:5–15).
> Jesus promised to save, keep, and resurrect to eternal life all who trust in Him (John 6:35–40).
> Jesus promised provision for our needs (Matthew 6:25–34).
> Jesus promised that He would give all we need to live for Him (2 Peter 1:3–4).
> We are assured we are saved (John 10:29).

So what is a conditional promise? "Promises that carry with them directions (conditions) that we must follow if we are to enjoy all that He has offered," according to De Haan. "These conditional promises are dependent on our fulfilling certain requirements."[4]

Conditional promises include:

> God promised success, prosperity, and protection *if* the people obeyed the Law of Moses (Joshua 1:7–9).
> *If* a person delights in the Lord, then He will give the desires of his heart (Psalm 37:4).
> *If* we seek what has eternal value, God will take care of our needs (Matthew 6:25–34).
> *If* we put our trust in Jesus, we will be given eternal life, but if we reject Him, we cannot escape condemnation (John 3:16–18).
> *If* we submit to God and resist the Devil, he will flee from us (James 4:7).
> God will forgive *if* we confess (1 John 1:9).
> *If* we pray according to His will, He hears and will do what we ask (1 John 5:14–15).

Psalm 145 offers good examples of some promises that apply to all God's people and then other promises that apply to a select group or person. Verses 9 and 16 hold promises for all of us: "The Lord is good to all, and he has compassion on all he has made.... You open your hand and satisfy the desire of every living thing."

Then come the promises to select groups: "The Lord is near to all who call on him, to all who call on him in truth. He fulfills the desires of those who fear him; he hears their cry and saves them. The Lord watches over all who love him, but all the wicked he will destroy" (verses 18).

Because God is a faithful God, we can bank on His promises, for He "is not a man, that he should lie, nor a son of man, that he should change his mind. Does he speak and then not act? Does he promise and not fulfill?" (Numbers 23:19).

A dear friend of mine, Leslie, gave a devotional at my daughter-in-love Bonnie's baby shower. Bonnie was to have her baby in a month, but we knew she was carrying a boy, whose name would be Joshua. At the end of Leslie's devotional, she handed out Scriptures from the book of Joshua for each of us to pray for my unborn grandson.

With confidence one mom prayed the *promise* of Joshua 1:5. "Dear loving Father, as You promised Joshua of old, I pray for Bonnie and Troy's Joshua that '. . . As you were with Moses, you will be with Joshua.' Thank You for the promise that You will never leave him nor forsake him" (Hebrews 13:5).

Another mom prayed this *conditional* promise for my grandson: "Father, I pray that Joshua will be careful to obey all the law your servant Moses gave, not turning from it to the right or to the left, so that he may be successful wherever he goes" (Joshua 1:8).

And yet another mom prayed a *conditional* promise for Joshua. "Lord, I pray that Joshua will not let this Book of the Law depart from his mouth; may he meditate on it day and night, so that he may be careful to do everything written in it. Then he will be prosperous and successful."

The outpouring of love for Joshua using God's Word so ministered to Bonnie that at a later date she keyed in the Scriptures on the computer, printed them out in a bold font, and framed each verse. Then she arranged the verses on the walls in Joshua's bedroom. Her desire was to tell Joshua how these women who didn't know him yet prayed God's very words for him. Bonnie plans to help him memorize each verse as he grows up.

God puts Himself within our reach when we say to Him, "Lord, You promised." He can't go back on His promise. Charles Spurgeon expressed it this way, "Every promise of Scripture is a writing of God, which may be pleaded before Him with this reasonable request, 'Do as Thou hast said!'"[5]

Susan was a mother who knew how to pray God's promises. She would go into her troubled teenage daughter's bedroom while her daughter was in school and cry out to the Lord for hours. "Pouring out my heart like water for the life of my girl, who was caught up in a life of drugs and rebellion" is how Susan puts it.

Susan prayed from the promises in Scripture that Dannika would love the Lord her God with all her heart and soul and mind and strength; that she would really know who she was in Christ, that she was fearfully and wonderfully made; that she would trust in the Lord with all her heart and lean not on her own understanding, but in all her ways acknowledge Him and He would direct her path; that God would soften her cold hard heart, remove her heart of stone, and replace it with a heart of flesh; that she would enjoy the companionship of those who love the Lord and have pure hearts; that she would hate what God hates; that lies would be far from her lips; that she would cry out to God and God would deliver her out of her distress, heal, and rescue her; that God would tear down the strongholds in Dannika's life (the drugs, the eating disorder, the unhealthy relationships, the foul mouth, the disobedience, the defiance, the dishonesty, and the disrespect).

Then Susan prayed for herself. She was not only going through tough times with Dannika, but she also had a troubled marriage and challenges with her three sons. "I drew comfort over and over from God's Word," Susan said, including, "Do not fear for I AM with you, do not be dismayed for I AM your God. I will strengthen you and help you."

"His promises continue to carry me and will until the day I see Him face-to-face," Susan says, as she tells how three years after beginning to pray fervently God's promises back to Him, Dannika accepted Christ and was baptized.

Susan couldn't have prayed as she did if she hadn't known what God's promises were. The same holds true for each of us. We can't pray God's promises for us, for our husbands, for our children, for our churches, or for our communities if we don't know what those promises are. We need to know the "whole" of Scripture so that we can proclaim with Jeremiah, "Your words are what sustain me. They bring me great joy and are my heart's delight, for I bear your name, O LORD God Almighty" (Jeremiah 15:16, NLB).

A powerful praying life is praying God's promises back to Him. Oh, that it might be said of us as was said of Abraham, "Yet he did not waver through unbelief regarding the promise of God, but was strengthened in his faith and gave glory to God, being fully persuaded that God had power to do what he had promised" (Romans 4:20–21).

I wavered a bit in my faith regarding my daughter, Trisha. Throughout her senior year in high school, I regularly prayed for her the promise found in Psalm 32:8, "I will instruct (Trisha), says the Lord and guide (her) along the best pathway for (her) life; I will advise and watch (her) progress." This Scripture brought peace to my heart, as she faced the huge decision of where to go to college. I had my own idea of where the Lord might send her. You see, a Christian college was located about forty-five minutes from our house, and I thought that would be a safe place for her to go. Since Trisha was the baby of the family and the only girl, I wanted her to be close, but I also desired for her an environment that had the same faith foundation she was raised on. But I sincerely prayed that God's will be done. Trisha visited several colleges, including the one forty-five minutes from our home.

As she was praying about it, I knew God would guide her and instruct her along the best pathway for her life. He would escort her in her every step.

Every time I wanted to doubt this promise, God would catch me in the safety net of His sovereignty. I remember one particular day when I was fretting, I read Acts 17:26–27. "From one man he [God] made every nation of men, that they should inhabit the whole earth; and *he determined the times set for them and the exact places where they should live.* God did this so that men would seek him and perhaps reach out for him and find him, though he is not far from each one of us" [italics mine].

The Holy Spirit so touched my heart with this wonderful truth that I immediately went to prayer, "Sovereign Lord, thank You so much for these comforting words, that wherever our children are You have placed them there. You have fixed beforehand the exact times and places where they should live so that the circumstances in which they find themselves will cause them to look for Jesus and find Him. Therefore, my Father, I do not need to worry or fear, for I can trust You, my sovereign God."

After that time of prayer, I was able once again to surrender my precious gift, my Trisha, to my trustworthy God. How did God answer my prayer? He chose to send her to a secular college ten and a half hours away from our home. And that is exactly the soil where her faith and intimacy with her beloved Jesus grew to new depths.

"Is Anything Too Hard for Me?"

Our faith increases as we pray God's promises and believe in the God who asks the rhetorical question, "Is anything too hard for me?" (Jeremiah 32:27). The Word emphatically states, "For with God nothing is ever impossible, and no word from God shall be without power or impossible of fulfillment" (Luke 1:37, AMP).

Let's pray against limited faith. Limited faith is controlled by our circumstances and motivated by fear. But unlimited faith fixes its eyes on Jesus, the author and finisher of our faith.

The story is told of a large earthquake, which caused the inhabitants of a small village to quake with fear. But they were surprised at the calmness and apparent joy of an old woman. At length one of the villagers addressed the old woman, "Mother, are you not afraid?" "No," she said. "I rejoice to know that I have a God who can shake the world."

It brings God great pleasure when we believe what He says and pray it back to Him, for "without faith it is impossible to please God, because anyone who comes to him must believe that he exists and that he rewards those who earnestly seek him" (Hebrews 11:6).

How do we get faith? Romans 10:17 tells us, "Faith cometh by hearing, and hearing by the word of God." God's Word helps our faith to grow.

How much faith do we have to have? Jesus gives the answer, "I tell you the truth, if you have faith as small as a mustard seed, you can say to this mountain, 'Move from here to there' and it will move. Nothing will be impossible for you" (Matthew 17:20). Isn't that awesome? It's not how much faith we have that matters but the object of our faith. God wants to show us "great and mighty things" as we ask according to His Word.

That was certainly true for a desperate wife who relayed to me about the stressful, unhappy marriage she was in. She had lost hope. Her husband wouldn't go to church or to a counselor. For years she had prayed for God to change him. She reached the point she had no feeling for her husband. She felt alone, betrayed, and spiritually dry.

The Lord spoke to her heart, as she read 1 Peter 3:1–2, "Wives, in the same way be submissive to your husbands so that, if any of them do not believe the word, they may be won over without words by the behavior of their wives, when they see the purity and reverence of our lives." She was convicted by the Word that her husband was not seeing a

> *It's not how much faith we have that matters but the object of our faith. God wants to show us "great and mighty things" as we ask according to His Word.*

pure and reverent life and that often her words were not gracious. He saw her be kind, courteous, and patient with everyone but him. She clung to this promise in 1 Peter and asked God to help her be the sort of wife Peter talked about.

She asked Jesus to love her husband through her because she couldn't. God heard her simple prayer, as she claimed that promise, and because her heart was open to God, He changed her. First, she chose to love her husband right where he was. She realized God alone could change a heart, not her badgering, coercing, and endless expectations. She kept a close watch on her mouth and instead began to pray Scripture for her husband. As she worked at strengthening her relationship with Jesus, she developed a sweeter spirit toward her husband, choosing to focus on his strengths and not his weaknesses, to compliment him, speaking words of affirmation and encouragement. Her faith increased, and she found it easier to believe that "the Lord is not slow in keeping his promise, as some understand slowness. He is patient with you, not wanting anyone to perish, but everyone to come to repentance"(2 Peter 3:9).

She said, "I figured if God was patient, I could be patient too. It took decades, but my husband is now a believer." As they attend church together and pray together, she rejoices in God's faithfulness to His promises.

Jill also found God faithful to His promises. She knew that neither she nor her children loved the Lord with all their heart, soul, mind, and strength. She said, "It was something you would never tell anyone because they would think you were perfectly awful, but in my heart, I knew it was true. I began to pray daily for my children and for me Ephesians 3:18, that we would 'grasp how wide and long and high and deep is the love of Christ.' Just this past summer, my cell phone rang and it was my son, Josh. He was all choked up and could barely talk. Of course I was alarmed, but then he said, 'Mom, I just wanted you to know that I am amazed at how much God loves me. Mom, He is so real, He is so real. Have you ever been just overwhelmed by that?' I hung up the phone and shouted for joy. Only through prayer could my children be so transformed and see God's love so clearly. It took prayer to take that truth deep into my son's life. It's as if praying the Word of God allows it to go deep into your spirit."

Julie admits that her faith was tested as she prayed Isaiah 61:3 for her teenage daughters, that they would be called mighty oaks of righteousness, a planting of the Lord for the display of His splendor. "Many times their behavior is directly opposed to my vision of their becoming 'mighty oaks of righteousness,'" Julie said.

Then one week her elder daughter, Cindy, had to decide if she wanted to attend a dance. At the last minute, she decided to go. (Her sister, Carole, already had decided to attend.) The day after the dance Carole confided to her mother that Cindy had danced inappropriately.

"I didn't want to betray my daughter's trust," Julie said, "but I did want to bring to light what Cindy had done. Instead, I went to the Lord in prayer rather than to discuss the situation with Cindy."

That Sunday Cindy said she wanted to get together with the wife of their youth leader because she had done something at the dance that was dishonoring to God. She already had confessed to God, but she just wanted to talk to someone about it.

"I was so thankful God had stopped me from dragging a confession out of her," Julie said. "I'm comforted knowing the Holy Spirit dwells in my daughter's heart. He speaks to her, convicts her, and guides her. Truly He is making my daughter into a righteous woman for the display of His splendor."

Let's Pray

Listed below are promises for you to claim. Other promises appear on pages 203–204.

Take one promise per day or week. Write the verse on a 3 x 5 card. If you would like, memorize it. On the back of the 3 x 5 card, answer the question, What does this verse mean to me? Then write a prayer reminding God of His promise.

Salvation: "For God so loved the world that he gave his one and only Son, that whoever believes in him shall not perish but have eternal life" (John 3:16).

New person: "Therefore, if anyone is in Christ, he is a new creation; the old has gone, the new has come!" (2 Corinthians 5:17).

Provision: "Until now you have not asked for anything in my name. Ask and you will receive, and your joy will be complete" (John 16:24).

Victory: "No temptation has seized you except what is common to man. And God is faithful; he will not let you be tempted beyond what you can bear. But when you are tempted, he will also provide a way out so that you can stand up under it" (1 Corinthians 10:13).

Forgiveness: "If we confess our sins, he is faithful and just and will forgive us our sins and purify us from all unrighteousness" (1 John 1:9).

Encouragement: "I have told you these things, so that in me you may have peace. In this world you will have trouble. But take heart! I have overcome the world" (John 16:33).

Purpose: "'For I know the plans I have for you,' declares the LORD, 'plans to prosper you and not to harm you, plans to give you hope and a future'" (Jeremiah 29:11).

Finding God: "You will seek me and find me when you seek me with all your heart"(Jeremiah 29:13).

Fear: "So do not fear, for I am with you; do not be dismayed, for I am your God. I will strengthen you and help you; I will uphold you with my righteous right hand" (Isaiah 41:10).

Peace: "You will keep in perfect peace him whose mind is steadfast, because he trusts in you" (Isaiah 26:3).

Confidence: "I can do everything through him who gives me strength" (Philippians 4:13).

Guidance: "I will instruct you and teach you in the way you should go; I will counsel you and watch over you" (Psalm 32:8).

When your requests go unanswered and you are discouraged, weary, and have lost hope, hold up your Bible to say, "Heavenly Father, You promised." Then read aloud the promise. Your hope will be restored.

Touching Heaven, Changing Earth

When we pray, we are touching heaven, changing earth. Speaker Ron Hutchcraft reminds us, "God has thrown open His storehouse to His children. He's unlocked His infinite resources and promised that our prayer of faith would unleash those resources and aim them at the need we have, the situation we face, or the person we love. When you are praying, don't ever forget—you really are touching heaven, changing earth."[6]

> **When we pray, we are touching heaven, changing earth.**

Often our prayer of faith in MITI is that our children would get caught when guilty. Talk about touching heaven, changing earth! When our children get caught, we believe it gives them a chance to pay attention to God and to be obedient to what He wants. Over and over I've seen children healed, restored, and forgiven because they had to face the consequences of their actions.

Paula says, "The first time my daughter skipped a class in high school, she got caught. A Christian who worked in the office saw her being detained and asked what had happened. My daughter shared her frustration that others continually skipped and weren't caught. The office worker commented that my daughter was sanctified (set apart) for God's use. Imagine my daughter's astonishment when I told her that we not only pray that our children get caught when guilty but earlier that week we also prayed those very words that the worker shared with her."

God's promises provide us with guidelines regarding how to pray when our weary minds and heavy hearts are at a loss as to what to request. And His promises help us to pray persistently, as we offer His Words back to Him again and again. Then, when those prayers are answered, all the glory goes to Him, the Author and Finisher of our faith.

I would like to close this chapter with an old hymn. The words are my prayer for you.

Standing on the promises of Christ my King,
Through eternal ages let its praises ring!
Glory in the highest I will shout and sing—
Standing on the promises of God.

Standing on the promises that cannot fail
When the howling storms of doubt and fear assail;
By the living word of God I shall prevail—
Standing on the promises of God.

Standing on the promises of Christ the Lord,
Bound to Him eternally by love's strong cord,
Overcoming daily with the Spirit's sword—
Standing on the promises of God.

Standing on the promises I cannot fall,
Listening every moment to the Spirit's call,
Resting in my Savior as my all in all—
Standing on the promises of God.

R. Kelso Carter

9. One-Accord Praying

Kerrie had a disturbing dream one night. Her daughter, Nichole, was asked by a beautiful young woman to walk across a bridge that was high above a concrete sidewalk. The woman said she needed to talk with Nichole. As Nichole started across, the bridge crumbled under her feet. She quickly grabbed onto the rail, as pieces of the bridge fell on the solid sidewalk below. The young woman laughed, and her countenance changed, revealing a distressingly ugly face. She had deceived Nichole. Kerrie ran onto the falling bridge, grabbed Nichole's hand, and struggled to hold on to her.

"I was afraid I would lose my grip," Kerrie recounts, "and then I felt a hand grab my hand. I had the strength to pull my daughter to safety. Then I felt more and more strength, and I looked behind me to see a chain of people holding on to each other as they helped me pull Nichole to safety. I knew who the people were; they were all the prayer intercessors in our lives."

When Kerrie awoke she realized her dream was about Moms In Touch. She said, "I am so grateful that other moms take the time to 'link' onto the chain of prayer for each other's children."

Moms often ask me, "Why do I need to get together with others to pray? I already pray everyday for my children." My response is that, first and foremost, praying together is scriptural. The Bible consistently portrays God's people coming together to pray, especially during a crisis.

Glenda can affirm the importance of having a prayer group when a crisis careens into a mom's life. Her daughter, Michelle, was twelve when she was diagnosed with leukemia and told she had 65 percent chance of surviving.

"At a time like that it's difficult to pray," Glenda admitted. "You just go numb and do the task before you. I sent up a lot of popcorn prayers, but I know the prayers of others are what held me up and gave me strength each day."

Because they lived in Alaska, Michelle and her mom went to Seattle for Michelle's medical treatment. For more than seven months, the prayer group in Alaska not only prayed for them but also for the rest of Glenda's family. And they brought meals to Glenda's two sons and husband.

One of Michelle's brother's bone marrow was a match, and a transplant for Michelle increased her chance of surviving. But Michelle still had a couple of times in which she almost didn't make it. The prayer group kept praying.

Eventually, Michelle and her mom returned home. Since Michelle needed a germ-free environment, Glenda's prayer group spiffed up the house before the patient and her mom arrived.

"This August, six years after Michelle was diagnosed, we went back to Seattle for a checkup," Glenda said. "We heard the long awaited word that Michelle is cured of her leukemia. We praise God—and thank Him for the prayer group that faithfully prayed us through our long siege with cancer."

A very different sort of siege took place in Scripture when three powerful armies, bent on destruction, were arrayed against King Jehoshaphat and the people of Judah. What did Jehoshaphat do? He called together his people from around the nation, young and old, to plead to God "in unity." The next day God fought the battle and destroyed the nation's enemies (2 Chronicles 20).

Later in Scripture, Jesus' disciples experienced an emotional crisis. After placing all their hopes and dreams in their Teacher, their Friend, they had witnessed His cruel death and then saw Him return from the dead only to leave them again, ascending to heaven in a cloud. They were confused. But they didn't go their separate ways. They needed each other. They needed to seek God together. So they gathered in an upstairs room and prayed, pouring out to God all that was pressing hard on their hearts. Acts 1:14 says, "These all continued with one accord in prayer and supplication" (KJV). Isn't it amazing that God turned the world upside down through a little bunch of frightened followers—who prayed together?

God takes our corporate prayers and answers them even when our faith is weak. King Herod ordered Peter arrested, put in prison, and heavily guarded. But the church earnestly prayed. "The night before Herod was to bring him to trial, Peter was sleeping between two soldiers, bound with two chains, and sentries stood guard at the entrance. Suddenly an angel of the Lord appeared and a light shone in the cell. He struck Peter on the side and woke him up" (Acts 12:6–7). Peter had such peace he slept deeply. Ordering Peter to dress, the winged messenger led Peter out of the cell, opened the prison's locked gates, and walked with Peter out onto the street.

> *Isn't it amazing that God turned the world upside down through a little bunch of frightened followers—who prayed together?*

A group of believing friends were praying at that very moment. How do we know? Because Acts 12 then says, "Peter came to himself and said, 'Now I know without a doubt that the Lord sent his angel and rescued me from Herod's clutches and from everything the Jewish people were anticipating.' When this had dawned on him, he went to the house of Mary the mother of John ... where *many people had gathered and were praying*'" (verses 11–12, italics mine). But when the answer to their prayers came knocking at their door, they told Rhoda, the servant, that she was out of her mind (verse 15).

I can identify with the disciples, can't you? Many times when God answers, I'm surprised.

Releasing Power

Deuteronomy 32:30–31 provides a picture of the power God releases when two or more gather together to pray. "How could one man chase a thousand, or two put ten thousand to flight, unless their Rock had sold them, unless the LORD had given them up? For their rock is not like our Rock, as even our enemies concede."

Pastor Ray Stedman explains the passage this way:

That is a strange ratio, isn't it? Logic would tell you that if one could chase a thousand, then two would chase two thousand—a remarkable accomplishment by any measure. But spiritual truth transcends mere logic and arithmetic! The Lord says that when two Christians get together and seek God's power, there is an exponential increase in the effect of their prayers! Two shall put not two thousand, but *ten thousand* to flight![1]

Just think, when you have a prayer partner, you become ten times stronger.

When a mother says to me, I have only one other mom to pray with, I sense her disappointment. But I say to her, "That's awesome! You're so fortunate." Often I share with her the passage in Deuteronomy to remind her how powerful two praying together really are. Prayer groups also can take several forms: a group of couples, neighbors, singles, moms ... whenever we find others who share our concerns and want to pray, we've found a prayer group.

Praying with others (or one other) is what I call "conversationally praying in one accord." What makes a good conversation? Attentive listening, taking turns, being aware of the other person's concerns, not monopolizing, and connecting on the same subject. In conversational, one-accord praying, each participant prays in the same manner as a good conversation.

Praying Aloud

One-accord praying is praying aloud. I know those who have never prayed aloud can find the prospect fearful. Rosalind Rinker in her book *Prayer: Conversing with God* gives us hope.

Anyone who belongs to Jesus Christ, confessing Him as Lord and Savior, can be delivered from fear of praying in public. The first step is to ask Him to deliver you from this fear. Read II Timothy 1:7. "For God hath not given us the spirit of fear; but of power, and of love, and of a sound mind." ... Go ahead and stumble in your prayers, go ahead and cry. Out of your very weakness your brother is made strong. . . . Out of this weakness your brother, hearing and observing that you are in no better state than he, becomes strong. He is encouraged by your so-called failures that he, too, may meet the Lord in his weakness. . . . If I pray a "spiritual" sounding, well-padded prayer of which I am proud, who is helped by it? Neither I nor my brother.[2]

You can talk to God as you would talk to the woman sitting next to you in the group. You're having a conversation with God. "The more natural the prayer," Rosalind Rinker notes, "the more real He becomes."[3] "Thees" and "thous" are optional—it's not language we generally use when speaking to one another. And it's not the beauty of your words that counts but speaking from your heart.

"I almost missed it!" Kari admits. "I basically was dragged to Mom In Touch by a well-meaning friend. I was worried I couldn't pray well. As a new Christian, I wasn't as good as these 'prayer warriors.' I'd make a fool of myself!

"Thanks to my new MITI friends, I now realize how wrong I was. MITI isn't about judging each other's ability to pray. It's about praying for our children. It's not about being eloquent. It's about praying for our children. It's not about impressing anyone. It's about praying for our children.

"I almost missed the opportunity to do the most important thing I can do for my children—set aside one hour per week to pray for them, their teachers, and their school.

"My heart still pounds, my cheeks still turn red, and my palms still sweat every time I pray aloud, but it doesn't matter. God is listening, and He is answering my prayers."

One of our MITI leaders in Thailand shares this remarkable story: "I invited a Thai woman who recently received Christ to come to MITI (which we call *Maah phu huang yai,* Mothers Who Care a Lot). After I introduced her to two women, she said quietly, 'You know, I've never prayed aloud before.' I replied, 'That is fine; just sit and listen if you want, but if you want to try and join us, prayer is just talking to Jesus in very simple phrases and simple words.' This dear sister prayed aloud during the praise time, the thanksgiving time, and also in the intercession time! When our time was over I asked, 'So what do you mean you don't know how to pray aloud?' She answered, 'As a Buddhist, I longed to pray aloud and say something to Buddha, but the words never came out of my mouth ... I have been a Christian for four days, and for this entire hour, the words of praise, thanksgiving, and asking God to help others just flowed out. I've never experienced anything like this!'"

Remember, one-accord praying is just talking to Jesus. Picture Him right in the middle of your prayer group.

Praying Subject by Subject

One-accord prayer means *praying one subject at a time*. In normal conversation, I might say, "Did you know that my husband lost his job this week? We're very anxious about the future." Would my friend reply, "My son Joey got an 'A' on his final in English and will graduate with honors next week"? This is not only insensitive, but it also isn't carrying on a good conversation. When a group prays in one accord, everyone concentrates on one subject at a time, praying back and forth about that subject as led by the Holy Spirit. One person can pray several times about the subject. But no one monopolizes the conversation. After the subject is exhausted, a silence might follow as the group waits on God to lead someone to the next subject. The new subject is then introduced through prayer—it isn't shared; it is prayed.

In Evelyn Christenson's classic, *What Happens When Women Pray,* she tells us, "As the participants learn to pray in one accord subject by subject, prayers gain momentum, and become more spontaneous.... When those in our groups become proficient in this method, their spiritual pulses will be throbbing together in such a way that each one will begin to sense the direction of the Holy Spirit when it is time to start a new subject."[4]

Nancy, for example, had a burden for her son. The group prayed for him until the Spirit moved them on to a new topic.

Nancy prayed, "Gracious heavenly Father, my son is dating a girl who isn't a Christian, and she is encouraging him to participate in ungodly activities. I ask that You would remove her from his life."

Second mom prayed, "Lord, open his spiritual eyes that he might see the destructive way in which he is going. I pray that he will want to please You."

A third mom prayed, "I agree, Father. Whatever it takes to stop him from further wrong decisions, we ask that You would intervene. May he have a heart that wants to please You."

Second mom prayed, "And Lord, we pray that You would save this girl. Your will is that none should perish. You died for her and love her. We ask for her salvation."

"It's so helpful to hear other moms pray for my child," Debbie, a mom active in MITI, said. "It helps me know how to cover all aspects of my child's need. They think of things I never would have thought of."

A Salvadoran mom testifies to the power of one-accord prayer. "My daughter, who is almost nineteen years old, didn't want to attend the youth meetings at our church, claiming the youth pastor was boring. I had been praying alone about this problem and hadn't seen any answers. But one day I decided to pray just for this matter with a dear friend, and two weeks later, my daughter told me she was going to the youth meeting. Almost two months have passed, and she has faithfully attended the meetings every Saturday evening, and she even has encouraged other youngsters to go."

Praying in Harmony

One-accord prayer is agreement prayer. Matthew 18:19–20 states, "If two of you agree (harmonize together, together make a symphony) about—anything and everything—whatever they shall ask, it will come to pass and be done for them by My Father in heaven. For wherever two or three are gathered (drawn together as My followers) in (into) My name, there I AM in the midst of them" (AMP). Agreeing in prayer means believers praying in harmony, with one heart and one mind, together under the direction of the Conductor, Jesus.

Sharon, a leader for her Moms In Touch group, felt "strongly impressed" by the Spirit to use a particular Scripture on healing in the intercession time for their children. "I remember being puzzled as to why this was so important," Sharon recalls, "because as far as I knew, the children we prayed for were all healthy. But I followed the Spirit's prompting. As we moms prayed for one child, the mom began to weep. Later she confided that her child was born with some physical and learning difficulties, and the Scripture I had prayed was the very Scripture the Lord gave her at the child's birth. It was as if God was confirming this promise to her. When we pray together in 'one accord,' time after time, the Spirit brings confirmation through our prayers. That is encouragement the world cannot give."

> *One-accord praying doesn't mean just agreeing with another's opinion or point of view but agreeing together about God's will—what He wants.*

If we want to pray Spirit-directed prayers, we must make sure that all known sin is confessed. That's why the second step in the four life-changing prayers, confession, is vital to praying powerful prayers of agreement. Then the Spirit can speak to our hearts and to the very heart of God. One-accord praying doesn't mean just agreeing with another's opinion or point of view but agreeing together about God's will—what He wants.

Praying Simply

One-accord prayer is making sure that prayers are brief, honest, and to the point. Have you ever been to a prayer meeting where one person "prays around the world," moving from topic to topic without giving others a chance to pray? Lengthy prayers cause people to disengage, unity to be lost, and minds to wander. More importantly, if one person does all the praying, the group misses out on what the Holy Spirit wanted to pray through another member of the body.

Keeping prayers brief—a sentence or two at a time—makes everyone feel more comfortable joining in. I encourage the KISS method of praying: Keep It Simple and Short.

Praying Specifically

One-accord prayer is praying scripturally and specifically. Specific prayers help us to sort out with the Lord what it is we're asking. Specific prayers remind us of James's wonderful admonition, "You do not have, because you do not ask God" (James 4:2). God wants us to be honest with Him, sharing what we need and desire, but always with a heart wanting His will over ours.

Paul is a wonderful mentor in teaching us to pray specifically. In Romans 15:30–31, he asks the church to continue to pray that God would deliver him. To the church of Colossae he asks them to pray that God would open a door for their message and that he would proclaim it clearly (Colossians 4:3–4). In 1 Thessalonians 3:10–11 he asks the church to pray that God would clear the way for him to come see them. Then he prays for the church members, that God would "fulfill every good purpose of yours and every act prompted by your faith" (2 Thessalonians 1:11) and that God would strengthen and protect them from the Evil One (2 Thessalonians 3:3).

Praying by using Scripture is powerful, for we are praying back to God His very words on behalf of those for whom we are interceding. A group might take a verse or portion of Scripture and pray that passage, asking God's power to intervene according to His Word.

The first pray-er might pray, "Heavenly Father, I pray for my daughter Philippians 2:15, that she will be blameless and pure, a child of God without fault in a crooked and depraved generation, in which she will shine like a star in the universe as she holds out the word of life."

Second pray-er: "Oh, Lord, I agree. Keep Sara from doing anything that would tarnish her reputation as a Christian."

Third pray-er: "Father, keep her close to Your heart and protect her from this crooked and depraved generation."

Second pray-er: "Yes, Lord, and I ask that You would give her courage to let her light shine for Jesus wherever she is. That she would unashamedly proclaim the truths in Your Word."

Praying as the Spirit Directs

One-accord prayer is Spirit-directed prayer. The Holy Spirit within us moves in our hearts, initiates our requests, and tells us how we should pray. The focus is on God and not on others' approval. This brings freedom to pray as we feel led and eliminates the fears that come with praying in a group. No one has to "take a turn." We join the conversation as the Holy Spirit prompts our hearts.

One mother confessed, "Plenty of times I've stumbled over my words and maybe didn't make complete sense when I spoke, but I came to understand that God accepted what I was offering, and I gradually learned to lean on the Holy Spirit's leading and to be focused on God, not on those around me."

Conversationally praying in one accord is a method of prayer that will revitalize and ignite your prayer group. One-accord, group prayer involves praying aloud; praying for one subject at a time; agreeing in prayer; keeping prayers brief, honest, and to the point; praying scripturally and specifically; and praying as the Spirit directs.

A Network of Strength

Keep in mind that we need to guard against divisiveness—anything that might creep into our prayer group that would cause disunity. God wants us to be unified, as Scripture reminds us. "May the God who gives endurance and encouragement give you a spirit of unity among yourselves as you follow Christ Jesus, *so that with one heart and mouth you may glorify the God and Father of our Lord Jesus Christ* (Romans 15:5–6, italics mine). Satan doesn't want unity because he knows that's how he is defeated. Alliance produces strength.

One-accord prayer creates a network of strength. We become like the giant redwood trees—strong, grand, and beautiful in their majesty. One would suppose that the redwoods' roots would go deep to support their tremendous height; but, in fact, the root system is shallow. These mighty trees connect to each other by their roots, with the roots of one intermingling with the roots of the others, to form a network of strength. Christians need to give one another "redwood support" through one-accord praying. As we unite in prayer, lifting one another's burdens, we will see new dimensions of God's strength.

Let's Pray

Finding a Heart Partner

In what area of your life do you feel the need for prayer support? Do you have a son or daughter in the military? Are you concerned about your children going to public school? Would you like to see your husband grow in his faith and be closer in his relationship with you? Is there a burden to pray for the pastors at your church? The media? The president and cabinet? Help in personal growth, such as losing weight or exercising regularly? *Ask God to bring to your mind another person(s) who has the same burden as you.*

Share with her your heart concerning the burden and ask if she would be willing to pray with you. Then make a commitment to meet at a specific time each week. I suggest using the four steps prayer format and the methods of praying in one accord shared in this chapter. It will keep you praying and not talking. Be intentional about meeting together, but if distance is a problem, you could pray over the phone. Burdens shared in prayer become lighter. Be in tiptoe anticipation of the answers.

Father, lay on my heart a prayer partner or group of partners who share my burden and want to pray with others. Cause our paths to cross and give us like hearts. Place in each of us a desire and a determination to pray over the matter. Thank You for Your provision. In Jesus' name, amen.

Sharing Burdens

Praying in one accord for each other's concerns also fulfills the mandate of Galatians 6:2, "Carry each other's burdens, and in this way you will fulfill the law of Christ," and of Philippians 2:4, "Each of you should look not only to your own interests, but also to the interests of others." What sorrow or burden weighs you down? When someone is praying with you, you feel strength and power. The unity of asking together is encouraging, uplifting, and healing to the heart and mind.

"Two can accomplish more than twice as much as one, for the results can be much better. If one falls, the other pulls him up; but if a man falls when he is alone, he's in trouble.... And one standing alone can be attacked and defeated, but two can stand back-to-back and conquer; three is even better, for a triple-braided cord is not easily broken" (Ecclesiastes 4:9, 10, 12, TLB).

Virginia reports this answer as her group prayed together: "Seven years ago, I began to lead a Moms In Touch group in a troubled inner-city high school. Eight mothers participated in the group, and when we prayed, we seemed to always have insurmountable issues to pray about. Our school of 1,500 teens was in the newspaper all the time, and the news generally was bad.

"Then God drew students' hearts to Jesus. A dynamic local youth ministry began to make inroads, and many unchurched students discovered Jesus' love and grew in their faith.

"The sons of two of our MITI moms played instrumental roles in founding and facilitating student-led prayer groups that meet before school each week. Many students who have taken a stand for Christ are in leadership positions on athletic teams and in the student body. Their witness was so great that last year an incoming freshman girl commented to her mother 'all the popular kids are Christians.'"

This group of moms brought "insurmountable" issues to God in one-accord prayer and then watched God change the school's spiritual climate.

Sometimes praying in a group together even results in unity among churches in a community. Vreni, who lives in Switzerland, witnessed just that. "In a small village a MITI informational meeting was being held, and the husbands wanted to attend. When asked why, they said they wanted to find out about this ministry that was bringing their wives together from all the different churches. They were amazed because the churches didn't support one another or get along."

As the women in this chapter can attest, one-accord praying is so much more than a number of individuals coming together to make requests of God. One-accord praying results in:

burdens becoming lighter
faith increasing through answered prayer
sincere support for each mom, who knows she isn't alone
a safe place to release fears
deep friendships
love for other moms' children
accountability in each individual's prayer life
greater caring for the lost
renewed hope in times of discouragement
learning to listen to others and to the Holy Spirit
peace and expectancy
unity in the Body of Christ
learning how to pray

Oh, Father, sometimes I feel so many hindrances to pray in a group, forgetting the benefits that await me. Help me to forge through my fears, my concerns, even my excuses. Remind me that truly my burdens become lighter when another person helps me to carry them. Gather me together with others, Lord, that we might experience the power of united prayer. In Jesus' name, amen.

10. *Get Ready for a Fight: Warfare Prayers*

Some years ago on a hot summer California day, a little girl decided to cool off by playing in the ocean. As she hurried to reach the cool water, she ran out of her family's beachfront cottage, leaving behind her flip-flops and towel as she went. Diving under the water and then resurfacing, she swam out to where the water was the coolest.

Her mother, who was watching from the house, saw a shark's fin break the water's surface. In utter fear, the mom ran into the surf, yelling to her daughter as loudly as she could and then swam toward her little girl. Hearing her mother's voice, the girl made a U-turn to swim toward shore.

It was too late. Just as the mother reached her daughter, the shark attacked. The mom grabbed her little girl by the arms as the shark snatched her legs. That began an incredible tug-of-war. The shark, which was about six-feet long, was much stronger than the mother, but the mother was much too passionate to let go. A fisherman, who happened to be in a boat nearby, heard the mother's screams, pulled out a rifle, and shot the shark.

Remarkably, after weeks in the hospital, the little girl survived. Her legs were cut to the bone. And on her arms were deep scars where her mother's fingernails had dug into her flesh as the mom hung on to the daughter she loved.

A television reporter who interviewed the girl after the trauma asked if she would show him her scars. The girl pulled back the hospital sheets. Then she said, "But look at my arms. I have great scars on my arms too. I have them because my mom wouldn't let go."

Like that mother who fought with a shark to save her daughter, we moms are fighting a spiritual tug-of-war with the enemy for our children. As my sister Gayle says, "Our children have beautiful scars because we're holding on to them for dear life through our prayers."

Fighting on Our Knees

A war is being waged for our children's hearts and minds. We must not passively sit back and allow Satan, called the thief in John 10:10, to steal, kill, and destroy our loved ones. We must respond with warfare prayers. The battle we wage for our children is on our knees. As 1 Peter 5:8 tells us, "Be self-controlled and alert. Your enemy the devil prowls around like a roaring lion looking for someone to devour."

One mom wasn't about to let Satan have her child. She relates how she prayed warfare prayers for him. He had accepted Christ as a young child, but during his teenage years drank, used drugs, and lived on the edge. This mom cried out to God countless times, "Father, You promise to deliver us from the Evil One." And then she would address Satan. "Satan, you can't have my son. He belongs to Jesus. I command you in the name of Jesus and in the power of His blood to release your grasp on Ben. Let him go! You have been fatally wounded at the cross. Jesus is the victor, and He has victory over you regarding my son."

> *The battle we wage for our children is on our knees.*

What I found most compelling as she told me her story was that, when she prayed, she didn't want a mediocre, lukewarm, sitting-on-the-fence, go-to-church-once-a-week son. She wanted Ben to fervently desire to serve in God's kingdom. Eight years later God answered the prayer just as she had prayed. Ben leads a Bible study and goes on missions trips. He preaches and shares his testimony. Many are coming to know the Lord and are being discipled because of Ben's surrendered life.

Yes, the battle for souls is intense and very real. Two kingdoms are involved: the kingdom of darkness, ruled by Satan; and the kingdom of light, ruled by Jesus Christ. All of us are in one kingdom or the other; we can't be citizens of both. When a person accepts Christ as Lord and Savior, that individual immediately is transferred from Satan's kingdom to God's kingdom. "For he [the Father] has rescued us from the dominion of darkness and brought us into the kingdom of the Son he loves" (Colossians 1:13).

The warfare doesn't end after our children give their lives to Jesus. Satan doesn't want them to live out the destiny God has for them; so we must stay in the fray on their behalf, as Candy did for her teenage daughter, Tiffanie.

"After I got saved," Tiffanie says, "I had to deal with the consequences of my bad choices. In my depression and confusion, I had stopped going to school regularly. When I decided to start over and get caught up, I was overwhelmed. I remember one time at school I was so far behind, I was freaking out, in tears. I went into the bathroom and pulled out a card my mom had given me. I read what she was praying. 'That Tiffanie would be strong and courageous and get to work. That she wouldn't be frightened by the size of the task, for the Lord my God is with her; He will not forsake her. He will see to it that everything is finished correctly (1 Chronicles 28:20).' God used that prayer to give me the courage to go on."

The Winner Is . . .

Despite our prayers, doesn't it seem at times that Satan is winning? At our Moms In Touch tenth-anniversary celebration, Evelyn Christenson told a gripping story that portrays how the war will end.

Mr. Das was a government administrator during British colonial rule in India at the turn of the century. In his work he traveled throughout the country. Since no hotels existed in remote areas, the British had provided strategically placed little houses to accommodate government workers.

On one occasion, Mr. Das and his entourage were traveling in the jungle south of Calcutta. With nightfall coming, he sent some men ahead to prepare the government house for their arrival. Suddenly, a servant came dashing out of the house, white as a sheet and incoherent. He had encountered a twenty-foot python curled around a piece of furniture.

A python can swallow a deer, a pig, or a human being whole. It is a deadly, powerful snake.

Mr. Das and his servants secured all the windows and doors, locking the python inside, and pulled out the ammunition box. Only one bullet was powerful enough to kill a snake of that size, and then only if the shooter hit its head.

Taking careful aim, Mr. Das shot the python right in the head, but to everyone's amazement, the python didn't die. Instead, it became crazed. It thrashed about, knocking down every light fixture, smashing every piece of furniture, and demolishing the interior of the house. The onlookers stood terrified, wondering if this crazed python would break out. Then, after an hour and a half, the snake died.

Mr. Das, who was also a great preacher, used to tell this story of the python and explain it like this: We, dear Christians, are living in that one and a half hours. Satan brought sin to planet Earth, tempted Adam and Eve, and man fell. But the Lord God said to Satan, that old snake, "I will put enmity between you and the woman, and between your offspring and hers; he [Jesus] will crush your head, and you will strike his heel" (Genesis 3:14–15). God had a "bullet" powerful enough to kill that serpent Satan. With His Son, Jesus, hanging on the cross, God the Father took careful aim, shot, and hit Satan right in the head.

Satan received the fatal blow at the cross, but for reasons we don't understand, God has permitted him to have another "hour and a half," as it were. With that bullet in his head, Satan is crazed. He is thrashing and smashing everything he can, trying to get each of us.

We are in the midst of a battle that is growing increasingly fierce, but don't ever forget that the fatal blow has been struck. Sometimes it looks as though Satan is winning, but he is not. He already has been defeated and will end up in the lake of fire forever and ever, while Jesus will be acknowledged as King of Kings and Lord of Lords.

The Foe's Battle Plan

Because we're living in that "hour and a half," we must know what tactics our foe uses. The Bible tells us: Satan is the accuser (Revelation 12:10); Satan is a murderer and a liar (John 8:44); Satan is a deceiver (Revelation 20:10); and Satan is a thief (John 10:10).

I haven't exhausted what the Bible says about Satan, but knowing these characteristics helps us to be "on alert" so we aren't taken by surprise or ambushed. They help us to know how to counterattack. And our counterattack isn't in the physical realm but in the spiritual realm. "For though we live in the world, we do not wage war as the world does. The weapons we fight with are not the weapons of the world. On the contrary, they have divine power to demolish strongholds" (2 Corinthians 10:3–4).

The first thrust of our attack is to pray in Jesus' name. We possess all power and authority to resist Satan in Jesus' name (Matthew 28:19–20). James 4:7 instructs us to "*Submit* yourselves, then, to God. *Resist* the devil, and he will flee from you" (italics mine). In submitting to God we look up, seeing the almighty, sovereign Creator of heaven and earth, and then we resist Satan, commanding him to leave, to "get lost." Through the Holy Spirit's power, we can oppose, strike back, stop, baffle, and frustrate Satan's opposition by praying in the authority of Jesus' name.

Now, most of us have been taught we are to end our prayers by saying, "In Jesus' name, amen." But have you ever wondered why we've received such instruction?

We conclude a prayer with that phrase because Jesus tells us to. John 14:13–14 says, "You can ask him [God] for *anything*, using my name, and I will do it, for this will bring praise to the Father because of what I, the Son, will do for you. Yes, ask *anything,* using my name, and I will do it!" (italics mine, TLB). I can't secure anything from the heavenly Father in my own name; it has no worthiness or authority attached to it.

When I attend the basketball games my husband coaches, I tell the ticket-taker I'm the coach's wife. Guess what? I get in free. Not because my name is "Fern," but because I belong to the coach and use his name. When we come before our heavenly Father, Jesus' name is our reference. Jesus is the divine "yes," the sovereign "amen," as we pray according to His will. His name creates expectancy, gives confidence, brings about miracles, breaks strongholds, sets captives free, heals the brokenhearted. All authority in heaven and earth are in His name (Matthew 28:18).

The second part of our strategy is to stand firm in prayer. Ephesians 6:10 admonishes us to "be strong in the Lord and in his mighty power." How? "Put on the full [whole] armor of God so that you can take your stand against the devil's schemes . . . so that when [not if] the day of evil comes, you may be able to stand your ground, and after you have done everything, to stand"(Ephesians 6:11,13).

A wonderful illustration of standing firm no matter what Satan may dish out is told by Pastor Tim Sheets.

> Jim Hester, a pastor in Arlington, Texas, tells the story about an old farmer who had a dug well. A dug well, from what I understand, is bigger around than a normal well because it has been dug by hand with a pick and shovel. This particular farmer had a prize mule that was his pride and joy. One day this mule fell into the dug well. The old farmer tried every way he could to get him out. He tried to hook ropes around him and pull him out, but the old mule was panic-stricken and would not let the ropes or anyone near him. Finally, after many hours of trying and many attempts, the old farmer gave up on retrieving his prize mule and decided to bury him right then and there. He and the men helping him got some shovels and started shoveling in the dirt on top of the mule in the bottom of the well. However, instead of allowing himself to be buried, that old mule began to scramble around on the dirt and stand on top of it. They'd throw some more in, and he'd do the same thing. Finally, he got high enough to just walk right out of that dug well.[1]

Tim then applies this illustration.

When we fall into one of the devil's wells and he attempts to bury us, we need to make a decision to stand like the old mule did. When Satan throws dirt in on us, we should scramble around on it and stand. As he continues to throw in more dirt, stamp it down and stand firmer. We are to let his stumbling blocks become our stepping-stones. Finally, when we've made the decision to stand, we can walk away from that well (or pit) a conqueror.[2]

Satan wanted to throw his dirt on a particular high school, but a group of women stood firm in prayer. One of the moms in the group tells the story like this: "As our high school prepared to celebrate Homecoming, the moms in our prayer group prayed, as we often had in the past, that our kids would be safe and that the students in the high school would make wise choices. Our group had been praying for years, and we thought we had the situation covered in prayer.

"But then we heard reports that shook our confidence. New drugs were being peddled and used throughout the school—and not just by those we had labeled as 'at risk.' Athletes, student leaders, cheer-leaders, and even professing Christians had been roped in.

"We moms wondered, have we been vigilant enough in our prayers? Did we fail to follow Christ's instructions to 'keep watch' so that we wouldn't be found sleeping? Shaken, but with renewed deter-mination, we turned to God and praised Him as our Rock and our Fortress. As we prayed, we began to see God not as a hiding-place kind of fortress, but as one that served as an arsenal of courage and strength in the battle that was before us."

For several weeks the women stood firm in their prayers, asking that the students would be convicted and freed from the bondage of drugs, that the staff and administrators would be bold like David as they confronted this "giant" of a problem, that other moms would become engaged in the battle and not grow weary, that all the parents would be convicted to seek God to guard their homes, and that the government leaders would have the wisdom and courage to legislate solutions.

A year since they stepped into the battle, the moms have seen a number of students join drug recovery programs while other students worked on a multimedia presentation to expose the dangers of the popular drugs. A school staff member became an energetic spokesperson about the threat of drugs, and an anti-drug event sponsored by the PTSA drew 250 parents as well as the mayor and representatives from the school board, sheriff's department, and city council.

"Best of all," this mom says, "the 3,300 students at the school heard a nationally renowned speaker challenge them to become the generation that would make changes. After his presentation, he met personally with a number of students, and thirty-eight kids accepted Christ. As moms, we may feel afraid or overwhelmed by the challenges our children face, but God is mighty!"

What does it mean to you to "stand firm" in prayer? How can you turn Satan's stumbling blocks into stepping-stones in your situation?

In addition to praying in Jesus' name and standing firm in prayer *the third part of our strategy is to recognize that the battle is spiritual, not physical.* The moms from the drug-infested high school weren't wrestling against flesh and blood "but against the rulers, against the authorities, against the powers of this dark world and against the spiritual forces of evil in the heavenly realms" (Ephesians 6:12). We aren't fighting against our husbands, our children, our situations, our schools—that's flesh and blood, what is seen—but we're fighting against the evil forces behind people or circumstances. Perhaps it would help you, when you pray, to visualize the spiritual aspects of the battle rather than picturing the individuals or the situations that *seem* to be the problem. That way your prayer focus will be on the evil forces that prevent spiritual progress.

> *We aren't fighting against our husbands, our children, our situations, our schools— that's flesh and blood, what is seen—but we're fighting against the evil forces behind people or circumstances.*

Even though we can't see the enemy, or what's happening in the spiritual realm, nonetheless our prayers cause spiritual turbulence. As soon as we utter a prayer, God is at work. Hebrews 1:14 informs us that ministering angels are commissioned on our behalf. "Are not all angels ministering spirits sent to serve those who will inherit salvation?" In Daniel 10, we're told that the answer to Daniel's prayer was delayed because the angel was resisted in warfare and couldn't bring the answer to him until twenty-one days later.

I don't understand all that happens on the spiritual plane when we pray Lord-You-must-do-something prayers, but Scripture reveals to us that our requests are earth- and heaven-shaking. God revealed to the disciple John a beautiful picture of what happens to the saints' prayers.

> Another angel, who had a golden censer, came and stood at the altar. He was given much incense to offer, with the prayers of all the saints, on the golden altar before the throne. The smoke of the incense, together with the prayers of the saints, went up before God from the angel's hand. Then the angel took the censer, filled it with fire from the altar, and hurled it on the earth; and there came peals of thunder, rumblings, flashes of lightning and an earthquake." (Revelation 8:3–5)

This description parallels what David describes in Psalm 18.

> In my distress I called to the LORD; I cried to my God for help. From his temple he heard my voice; my cry came before him, into his ears. The earth trembled and quaked, and the foundations of the mountains shook; ... He parted the heavens and came down; ... He reached down from on high and took hold of me; he drew me out of deep waters. He rescued me from my powerful enemy. (verse 6–7, 9, 16–17)

Never doubt God's powerful response to your prayers. Even though you might not see anything happen in the physical realm, believe that something is happening in the spiritual realm when you face the enemy. Things are shaken!

The fourth part of our prayer strategy is to have faith, even when we can't see the answers to our requests. I'm so glad God put the story about Elisha and his servant in the Bible. It assures us that activity is going on in the unseen world. The Aramean army was sent to capture the prophet Elisha, and his servant was fearful of what would happen to his master. As the servant stepped out of their sleeping quarters to see if the army was coming, what he saw must have set his heart to pounding even harder. Mighty soldiers, strong horses, and glistening chariots surrounded the city. But Elisha saw something different. He told his servant, "Don't be afraid. Those who are with us are more than those who are with them." Then Elisha prayed a faith-believing, intercessory prayer for his servant. "Oh, Lord, open his eyes so he may see."

God opened the servant's eyes, and this time he saw the hills outside the city full of horses and chariots of fire protecting him and Elisha. I can only imagine the look on the servant's face (2 Kings 6:12–23).

What a wonderful reminder to you and to me to "fix our eyes not on what is seen, but on what is unseen. For what is seen is temporary, but what is unseen is eternal." Isn't this the kind of "sight" you desire as God's child, the sight of one who is filled with faith? Then, when, like Elisha's servant, you "step out" (look past the person or situation you're praying about), you will see with eyes of faith.

Our fifth strategy is to put on the full armor of God. Are you equipped? Ready to win the battle? Paul tells us, "Therefore put on the full armor of God, so that when the day of evil comes, you may be able to stand your ground, and after you have done everything, to stand" (Ephesians 6:13).

When my son Travis played high school football, not once did I see him or his teammates run out to the field without wearing their football gear. I'm sure they never said, "Hey, it's too much work to put on all this equipment. Let's just play in our T-shirts, jeans, and tennis shoes."

While none of us would think of leaving our homes without getting dressed or just wearing our belt, so none of us should think about engaging in spiritual warfare without putting on the armor God has provided.

But Pastor Charles Stanley reminds us that knowing about the armor isn't a magic solution. Memorizing the parts of the armor will help you to "put on" each piece as you begin your day.[3] The armor is God's complete and total provision to wage spiritual warfare effectively.

Would you take a minute to pray on the armor? We might as well get in the habit now.

Suggested prayers:

To Begin

Heavenly Father, thank You that it's Your will for me to be strong in You and in the power of Your might. I rejoice that by faith I can put on the armor that You have provided for me to protect me from Satan's tactics and schemes. For my struggle is not against flesh and blood, but against the rulers, against the authorities, against the powers of this dark world and against the spiritual forces of evil in the heavenly realms.

Now, Lord, through Your Son I put on the full armor so that when the day of evil comes, I will be able to stand my ground. By Your unlimited grace, help me to withstand Satan's attacks.

Belt of Truth

Stand firm then, with the belt of truth buckled around your waist. (Ephesians 6:14)

Dear Jesus, I put on the belt of truth. I pray today that I will act with integrity in all my ways, speaking the truth. Keep me from saying or even intimating anything that isn't true. Help me to discern and recognize Satan's lies. May there be no hidden deception or impure motives found in me. I ask that the truth I speak to others will be lived out in my own life. I desire to live every moment only by the truth of Your words.

Breastplate of Righteousness

... with the breastplate of righteousness in place. (Ephesians 6:14)

Thank You for Christ's righteousness, given to me at the moment of salvation. Because of this wonderful gift of sal-

vation, I stand before You covered with the blood of Jesus, and I marvel in the truth that You see me as perfect. I rejoice that You don't view anyone who loves You as guilty. Help me to please You in everything I do. I pray I won't be stubbornly proud, which would keep me from confessing my sin the moment the Holy Spirit reveals it to me. Thank You that the breastplate gives me courage to know that Satan has to retreat from those who walk righteously.

Gospel of Peace

... and with your feet fitted with the readiness that comes from the gospel of peace. (Ephesians 6:15)

Dear Sovereign God, how awesome that I have peace with You because of Jesus. Nothing is more wonderful than to know that all is well between my God and me. It is a blessing beyond words. The assurance of eternal life brings sweet peace to my soul. Thank You for Your promise that You will give me Your peace if I will not be anxious but will tell You my needs. Thank You for the peace it brings to know that the Jesus in me is greater than he that is in the world. I shout for joy that in the midst of a shaken world, I can stand steadfast on these truths, putting Satan under my feet.

The Shield of Faith

In addition to all this, take up the shield of faith, with which you can extinguish all the flaming arrows of the evil one. (Ephesians 6:16)

My faithful God, thank You for the promise that the shield of faith extinguishes all the devil's flaming missiles. You are my shield. At Calvary You took the arrows that I deserved. Help me to have faith in You and You alone. I desire an unwavering trust that You not only can deliver but You also will deliver me from the Evil One's attacks. Thank You for the promise that the Enemy can't thwart Your plans for me. Father, help me when Satan's doubts and accusations come flying toward me, to hold up my shield of faith and to defeat him with the truth of Your Word.

The Helmet of Salvation

Take the helmet of salvation. (Ephesians 6:17)

Dear Lord and Savior, I rejoice in the assurance of my salvation. I thank You that because I am saved I have been given the mind of Christ. Thank You that the helmet of salvation protects and covers my mind from Satan's accusations and assaults. Help me to renew my mind with the transforming power of Your Word, so that, when Satan comes against me with his lies, I will not be disarmed. I want to have right thinking. Let me think Jesus' thoughts and discern His will in all things. I ask that You would guard my thoughts and vain imaginations. May my every thought be captive to the obedience of Christ. I submit my mind, my will, and my emotions to the authority of Your Spirit. I exalt Your holy name for the helmet of salvation, for Satan is defeated when he comes against a "saved" mind.

The Sword of the Spirit

And the sword of the Spirit, which is the word of God. (Ephesians 6:17)

Dear Gracious Father, I thank You for the infallible trustworthiness of Your Word. May Your Word dwell in me richly. May it be sweeter than honey to my mouth. I ask that Your Holy Spirit would give me an insatiable love for Your Word. Lord, I pray against those things that would keep me from reading and obeying Your Word. Help me to hide Your Word in my heart so when I'm tempted I can silence Satan with the words that Jesus used, "It is written ..." Your Word is sharper than any two-edged sword, and I anticipate great victories when I use it. I celebrate that Satan must retreat when Your Word is applied against him. Hallelujah!

Isn't it interesting that the sword of the Spirit is the last piece of armor listed in Ephesians? Perhaps that's because it is the only offensive weapon in the armor. It's the living Word, powerful, effective, and instructive. To be victorious, we must use it in the battle.

Now that you're wearing the armor, what does Paul tell you to do? Pray! "And pray in the Spirit on all occasions with all kinds of prayers and requests. With this in mind, be alert and always keep on praying for all the saints" (Ephesians 6:18). Prayer isn't the preparation for the battle; it *is* the battle.

Putting on the armor with her prayer group was one mom's source of power for faith-believing prayer. When Kathy's son was a junior in high school, he developed debilitating depression. He was accused of something he wasn't involved in, and one of his teachers targeted him for regular ridicule in front of the class. One morning he couldn't get out of bed and told her, "Mom, I feel as though I'm twelve feet under, and people are looking at me, but nobody wants to help me. I can't get my breath."

Kathy and her husband sought a Christian counselor for their son. The counselor's nonjudgmental support began to offer them some hope that their son could find his way out of his depression. To help him further, they moved him to a new school, where he would have a chance to "start over."

But Kathy feels the most important action was battling in prayer for her son. Her prayer group's coleader gave her a Scripture passage that showed God would fight for her son. "He reached down from on high and took hold of me; he drew me out of deep waters. He rescued me from my powerful enemy, from my foes, who were too strong for me. They confronted me in the day of my disaster, but the LORD was my support" (Psalm 18:16–18).

Kathy showed the verses to her son and said, "Honey, when you feel depressed, all you need to know is that God has His hand outstretched, and He will pull you up."

The struggle isn't over for this family, but Kathy's son believes prayer is powerful and that God can rescue him when he is assailed by the Enemy. Slowly, he is coming out of his depression, and Kathy continues to battle for him through prayer.

Like Kathy, we need to have a well-planned prayer strategy to fight Satan and his wily ways. That strategy includes: pray in Jesus' name, stand firm in prayer, recognize the battle is fought on the spiritual plane rather than the physical, have faith, and put on the full armor—every day.

"But man is born to trouble as the sparks and the flame fly upward," Job tells us. All moms hope for the best for their children, but the wise mother suits up with God's armor. His armor enables us to enter into the battle for our children when they encounter trouble and when we fight Satan over them to keep them from trouble. God's Word promises us victory. Ultimately, the desire of each of our hearts is that we would fight the good fight, that we would deserve the title, "prayer warrior."

> *Lord, help me to be diligent to put on the armor, realizing that it equips me to have a powerful prayer time, to come boldly before You. When I feel battle-weary, help me to realize that victory is mine through You. May I find ways to communicate to my children the importance of their being suited up in the armor. May I know that You have not given me "a spirit of timidity but a spirit of power, love, and self-discipline. . . . [And enable me to] endure hardship like a good solider of Christ Jesus" (2 Timothy 1:7; 2:3). In Jesus' name, amen.*

11. *Praying for Our Schools*

Denise, a second-grade public school teacher, assigns three students each day to stand up and share something they think is special. Most bring props of some sort to talk about.

One Monday a little girl took her turn. Walking to the front of the class, Moriah was beaming, but her hands were mysteriously empty. Denise asked Moriah if she was ready to share, and Moriah nodded yes.

Then she explained that God was the special thing she wanted to share. She told everyone how she had given her heart to Jesus and how it made her feel special to spend time with Him. How special it was to have God to talk to at night. How special to have God promise that she would live forever in heaven and how He was building a house just for her.

The last thing Moriah said she wanted to share was her favorite song about God. In a small, slightly off-tune voice, she sang "Our God Is an Awesome God." She barely had begun, when much to Denise's amazement, almost the entire class stood and sang along with her. Hands were lifted in worship all over the room, until even the kids who didn't know the song had their hands up too.

Denise said, "All I could do was weep, as I saw the children singing together. They were praising God in my classroom." When they had sung the song three times over, the kids broke into cheers.

Moriah and her classmates were declaring in song that Almighty God reigns in power, wisdom, and love. And to think that happened in a public school! As long as those who love Jesus are on our campuses, light is in those schools. How I thank God for all the Moriahs in our schools who love Jesus and want to share Him with others.

No Hope but Prayer

Yes, public education has problems, but God hasn't given up on our schools, and neither should we. According to the National Center for Education, more than forty-seven million children in 2001 attended public school.[1] Who will pray for all those children? Moms will. You can effect the spiritual and moral climate of the schools your children attend through prayer.

Dr. James Dobson, president of Focus on the Family, states, "When you look at the problems in schools today, when you look at the level of violence, things the kids see outside of class, things that are occurring on network television that are absolutely in the gutter, when you see all of this, there is no other solution, no other hope but prayer, and that's what brings you to your knees."[2]

How Praying Moms Can Change Schools

Moms are the prayer wall of protection around our schools. We identify with Nehemiah and the sorrow he felt over having walls in ruins. He actually wept as he heard that Jerusalem's walls were in shambles. Why? The walls in biblical times provided strength and protection. Fortified walls meant that the enemy couldn't penetrate into the city. With the walls broken down, Nehemiah knew Jerusalem was open to the enemy, vulnerable, helpless, in shame and disgrace. The rest of the world looked at Israel as having a weak God.

As we look at our schools today, we can see that the spiritual walls have been torn down. Even though we may build bigger and better school buildings, the spiritual walls lay in ruin. The Enemy has free access to our campuses. Does it make us weep as it did Nehemiah when he saw the destruction?

Praise God, like the walls of Jerusalem, our school walls can be rebuilt through the power of prayer. Picture with me, moms from every nation, people, and language, gathering together, standing shoulder-to-shoulder, arm in arm, forming a fortified wall of prayer. Each mom taking her position on the wall to counter Satan's attacks against that school. You are needed. For every part of the wall must be protected. No gaps, no missing bricks.

God says, "I looked for a man among them who would build up the wall and stand before me in the gap on behalf of the land" (Ezekiel 22:30). What a privilege to build up the wall, to stand in the gap, on behalf of our schools. "Repairer of broken walls"—isn't that a wonderful title to have as a mom? (Isaiah 58:12).

Praying moms have begun "this good work [prayer] . . . work[ing] with all their hearts" (Nehemiah 2:18; 4:6). Paul calls prayer "work" when he affirms his dear friend Epaphras. "He is always wrestling in prayer for you, that you may stand firm in all the will of God, mature and fully assured. I vouch for him that he is working hard for you" (Colossians 4:12–13).

Just as the enemy came against Nehemiah, taunting and ridiculing that the wall couldn't be rebuilt, likewise the Enemy comes against us to discourage us from this great task. But God will frustrate Satan's plans, if we will not give up our post on the wall.

What should you pray? How do you add bricks to the wall? Following, in *italic* type, are some suggested prayers. That's the work we are called to, simply—and powerfully—to pray. Following each prayer I've recounted examples of how God has responded in schools for which moms have prayed. Let each story encourage your heart that, in your child's school, God wants to use you as a "bricklayer."

> ***Lord, I ask that you would bring together Christian young people to proclaim Your name.***

Holy Father, protect them by the power of your name—the name you gave me—so that they may be one as we are one. (John 17:11)

Many moms who send their children to public school are fearful. Terri shares how she found peace concerning her son. "My oldest has been in Christian school and home-schooled, but this year we've been praying about sending our children to public school. We've been fearful about public school and the effect it would have on our children. But who will be the light to these children when all the Christian parents are pulling their children out? We're believing our children will change the children around them, not the other way around."

And God is uniting the Christian kids not only at their campuses but He is also bringing high school and college-age students together through citywide rallies and national conferences. In 2000 in Los Angeles and Washington, D.C., twenty thousand kids made decisions to be "campus missionaries" with a resounding shout of "I will go!"

At Chico State in California an evangelistic campaign was organized by several parachurch organizations. "I agree with Rich," proclaimed orange T-shirts that more than four hundred students wore for a week. The campaign culminated with Rich Thompson, a junior, sharing his testimony at the free speech area on campus.

But opposition arose, and a parody making fun of the campaign appeared on the Internet. The creators of the parody urged students to be at the free speech area to voice their opposition.

Moms prayed that God would give the four hundred students with the T-shirts the courage to wear them every day and asked that God would give Rich the ability to proclaim the truth with humility, boldness, and clarity. And that there would be no opposition.

Between seven hundred to nine hundred students gathered in the area and quietly listened as Rich spoke. Seeds were planted in hearts, and the opportunity was given to receive Christ that day. And the Christians faithfully wore their orange T-shirts.

Christians on other college campuses adopted the idea of using T-shirt campaigns. "Body Piercing Saved My Life" T-shirts were seen at Easter on the University of California, Davis campus. "Who Do You Think I Am?" T-shirts, based on Luke 9:20, proclaimed Christ at the University of California, Santa Barbara. A church college group was allowed to meet on one campus, and two hundred kids showed up. And moms prayed each time.

Pray for your children to be bold in speaking about their faith. Ask that they would present the good news of Jesus' resurrection to their classmates in loving and sensitive ways.

Father, I ask that this next generation, including my
child, will be a praying people and that they would stand
boldly for You on their campuses.

And pray in the Spirit on all occasions with all kinds of prayers and requests. With this in mind, be alert and always keep on praying for all the saints. (Ephesians 6:18)

See You At The Pole began in 1990 with thirty-five students in Texas. Millions of kids now gather around their flagpoles praying, "Oh, God, give us a passion for You; save our friends; protect us from the evil one; protect our school."[3]

At a school in California a young man brought two hundred to three hundred "Connecting with God" booklets published by Campus Crusade for Christ to his school's See You At The Pole event. He explained to the pray-ers that they should give the booklets to their friends, if they asked why they were praying. All the booklets were taken, and throughout the day, he saw kids giving them to their friends. The Gospel was scattered all over the campus that day.

Five committed Christian guys meet weekly to pray for their unsaved friends and peers. When one of them accepts Christ, the guys circle that person's name in red and then add another name to pray for.

Spontaneous prayer broke out in Mississippi when a few students at a football game held hands in the bleachers and began the Lord's Prayer. By the time they got to "deliver us from evil," 4,500 people had joined them.

Prayer is sweeping the hallways of our high schools, as students kneel by their lockers, praying for thirty seconds for their school. Tom Sipling, who founded the 30-Second Kneel Down, says, "I believe we're just going to see unbelievable supernatural events take place through this generation."[4]

Christians are starting prayer groups in dormitories and fraternity houses with the goal of covering every student on campus with prayer. The students at a Florida college are out to change its reputation from a party school to a prayer school.

What could happen at your child's school?

Father, I ask that our school be directed by biblical values and high moral standards; may Your Word come back into my child's classroom.

I wait for the LORD, my soul waits, and in his word I put my hope. (Psalm 130:5)

The National Council on Bible Curriculum offers state-certified Bible courses for public high schools. The Supreme Court has ruled that using the Bible as a textbook for history and literature is legal. As a result, more than eighteen thousand high school students in twenty-eight states have taken this elective Bible course.[5]

In Fort Gibson, Oklahoma, the sixty-six books of the Bible are now on the Accelerated Reader book list at a public school, and forty Bibles were needed in the library because of the demand. All this through the efforts of two fourth-grade girls and their Christian teacher. "The Bible was an immediate hit with the children," the teacher said. "It's not unusual to see Bibles at recess or in the cafeteria. They take the Bibles home and discuss it with their parents."[6]

Biblical truths are also coming back into the classroom through Eric Buehrer's ministry, Gateways to Better Education. This organization has created "The Holiday Restoration Cards" to help teachers understand how the religious aspect of Thanksgiving, Christmas, and Easter can be taught in the classroom.

A Californian mom writes, "Last night at our junior high PTA meeting our principal announced that our school district superintendent and the school board have decided that the Golden Rule (Matthew 7:12) should be printed and placed in each classroom within the district. They also have decided to integrate the 'Character Counts' curriculum, and my child's junior high principal showed me three Scriptures that were being reviewed for publication in the monthly district bulletin."

At Central Cabarrus High School in Concord, North Carolina, the guidance counselors had to tell one hundred students they couldn't take Bible classes this year. The reason? The classes were full.[7]

What specific prayers might you pray that could bring Christ's influence back to your child's school? What challenges are forefront that need to be addressed in prayer?

> *Father, I ask that my child will stay pure until marriage and that abstinence would be taught in the classroom.*

Do not be yoked together with unbelievers. (2 Corinthians 6:14)

It is God's will that you should be sanctified: that you should avoid sexual immorality; that each of you should learn to control his own body in a way that is holy and honorable, not in passionate lust like the heathen, who do not know God; and that in this matter no one should wrong his brother or take advantage of him. (1 Thessalonians 4:3–6)

What a thrill when the True Love Waits campaign was enthusiastically embraced by thousands of young people vowing to remain sexually pure.

When Jan's daughter entered womanhood, Jan took her thirteen-year-old to a nice lunch and rejoiced with her over the privilege of being a woman and God's preparing her body to be a mother someday. Jan encouraged her to make a covenant with God that she keep herself pure until marriage. The promise would be sealed with a ring. The daughter agreed. After lunch Jan took her to a store to pick out a ring that she would wear until her wedding night. On that night she would give her husband the ring, symbolizing that she was his gift to be unwrapped only by him.

Jan said, "Much prayer was given on her behalf to keep her promise to the Lord. And keep it she did, giving her groom the ring on their wedding night."

During Lin's involvement in the PTA in the late 1980s, she became aware of a new state law that required all sex education curricula be taught from an abstinence only perspective, rather than from a safe sex perspective. She asked her prayer group to pray for her as she brought this new law to the school board's attention.

The school board asked her to be on the committee to oversee the implementation of the law. In this capacity she evaluated every video and publication that currently was used in the sex education curriculum. Many of the materials didn't fulfill the law's requirement. As she brought her findings to the board, some of the members were shocked by the materials the district had been using.

Today this school district is among 33 percent of the districts nationwide that use an abstinence-only curriculum in sex education. That means students are not told how to use condoms or where to get birth control. They are taught to abstain from sexual intercourse until they are ready for marriage. Contraception is discussed only in its failures, and the students are reminded that abstinence is the only 100 percent effective method of birth control. Lin attributes the curriculum's adoption to the moms who faithfully prayed for her throughout her involvement.

Become aware, if you aren't already, of what your school is teaching your children. Use the information you gather as a source of specific prayer.

Father bring encouragement to the teachers through my words and deeds, but mainly through my prayers.

And whatever you do, whether in word or deed, do it all in the name of the Lord Jesus, giving thanks to God the Father through him. (Colossians 3:17)

This testimony really touches my heart: "For the last five years, I have taught in a school which has been turned around by the power of prayer. During my first year, . . . we all felt physically and emotionally beaten down—teachers and students alike. Then something wonderful happened. A handful of Christian moms from our school began a prayer group. There was a noticeable difference in the atmosphere of the school as a result of the prayers."

Almost always the school staff see praying moms as friends and look to us for prayer. Linda shares one of her favorite answers to prayer. "One of our moms was talking on the phone with a school staff member prior to our praying. The staff member asked us to pray for a drug situation. The staff knew of twelve students dealing drugs at the school but hadn't been able to catch them in the act or to document any evidence. We were asked to pray that the school would catch them.

"We went right to prayer. We prayed for these young people to get caught, asking the Lord to expose the darkness. We also prayed that they would come to know Jesus as their personal Savior.

"That evening one of our moms received a phone call from the staff member who had asked us to pray. 'You ladies have a hotline to heaven. Within fifteen minutes after I asked you to pray, a student came to tell us where the drug dealers were.'

"The city police and the school security surrounded the house where all twelve drug dealers and several students were doing drugs. They were all arrested and taken to the juvenile justice center."

Many young people at the justice center were coming to know the Lord through a staff worker. So God put the new detainees in a place where they could hear about Him.

Father, I ask that You will meet the needs of troubled children through their teachers or other sources.

I will search for the lost and bring back the strays. I will bind up the injured and strengthen the weak. (Ezekiel 34:16)

For two weeks my son Travis was the substitute teacher for a detention class of sixth graders, children stuck in a trailer away from the main campus. The forgotten kids. The outcasts. The troublemakers. The bad kids. When Travis shared stories about these children, it made me heartsick: foul language pouring from their mouths, some on drugs, dangerous, rude, disrespectful, low self-esteem, and so lost.

Not every child has a mom who will pray for him or her. Recently I spoke to about three hundred high school students at a Christian youth conference. "There may be some of you here who don't have a mom who prays for you," I said. "If you would like prayer, I would be honored to pray for you individually." After the meeting, I was amazed to see many young people stand in line to receive prayer from a surrogate mom.

Tears flowed as they shared their stories of unsaved moms and strained relationships. I'll never forget one young man who asked me to pray that he wouldn't hate his mom. He sobbed as I prayed for him.

Does your child's school have a class of troubled children? How many children in your child's school have no one to pray for them?

What a powerful prayer opportunity for you. You could pray that the light of Jesus would shine, penetrating that dark room of troubled children. Pray for the children's salvation. Pray that God will provide a teacher or an aide with wisdom, strength, and love for the unlovely children. Pray for the regular teacher, struggling with these children day after day. Pray for the children who need the attention of a praying mom, that God would encircle them with His love and that they would know He is present and caring for them.

Father, I ask that You would bring Christian teachers and staff together to pray.

For where two or three come together in my name, there am I with them. (Matthew 18:20)

Julie, a Christian teacher, shares how a teachers' prayer group started for her school. "Meeting to pray on the National Day of Prayer opened up the question, why not continue to pray on a regular basis? One of my friends had been involved in a MITI group, and I thought, why couldn't we do the same except we would be teachers praying for each other and the students? Each week we have about twenty-two staff gather together to pray. Every week through our time of prayer God affirms our call to love our students and help them to see how wonderful they are and the marvelous plan that God has for them. This is our mission field, and it's prayer that unleashes God's power to work in the lives of our students.

"When my daughter's school started a MITI group, I was quick to join and was sent a card that read, 'If you are not praying for your child, who is?' At my school I can say, 'The teachers will!'"

The amazing part of being a repairer of the breaches in our schools' walls is that the prayers rebound in ways one would never expect.

A Washington mom tells this story: "A walled pathway leading to our high school had become a hangout for gangs. Our prayer group had prayed for four years that God would do something about the gangs. God answered. The gang members got in trouble for all the graffiti they had painted on the pathway wall and were ordered to clean it up. When the husband of one of the moms in our group learned about the order, he suggested that he and some friends join the gang in helping them clean it up.

"The gang members didn't know how to respond when the group showed up and helped them to scrub and repaint. As all of them worked side by side, the young men began to drop their guard, and some shared about the painful things that were going on in their lives.

"By the time the helpers pulled out donuts and cocoa, God had softened many of the kids' hearts, setting the stage for the answer to a gang member's question, 'Why are you being so kind?'"

The gospel was shared, and true to God's promise, His Word didn't return void. Attitudes began to change, some gang members sought out counseling, and others began to develop more positive behaviors.

"It's been six years since this occurred," the mom continued, "and we've had no problems with gangs in our high school."

I hope all of the events I've recounted encourage you to pray vigorously and regularly for your child's school. It makes all the difference in the curriculum, in the spiritual environment, in the way children are dealt with, and in their futures.

Eric Buehrer from Gateway to Better Education expresses his optimism for public schools: "We stand at the threshold of great opportunities in our public schools. When I look out on tomorrow, I see a sun rising, not a sun setting. I see classrooms enriched by the appropriate expression of Christian values and ideas. I see children and young people—for the first time in their lives—gaining a new respect and appreciation for the contributions Christianity has made to America, the world, and their own lives. With God's grace and guidance, we can change the course of history."[8]

How Praying for Schools Changes Moms

God changes you when you pray for your child's school. You can widen your world beyond your family; feel more compassion for the teachers and administrators; find yourself involved in school issues in positive ways; and realize that you are not helpless, you can make a difference.

Karen says, "When you pray for a school, your love and concern expands beyond your family and circumstances. As you pray for individual students, teachers, and administrators, it gives you love for every one of them."

One mom grumbled and complained about how she hated the principal at her child's school. But as she became involved in praying for the school, she found she could work with the principal in a whole new way.

Raylene tells of the changes that took place in her life. "I'm witness to the blessing of my own personal growth since we started our prayer group. I'm excited and have a renewed purpose in being a full-time mom. I have a fresh love for my husband, and a new outlook on keeping house—to make it the place that each member of my family would most want to be."

Now, I can't promise everyone that praying for your school will make you want to be a better housekeeper! But I receive countless letters in which women express how praying for change in their school has changed them.

Bernie shares his story of the effect his wife had on him as she learned to pray in MITI. "I am not a mother, a student, or a teacher, and yet Moms In Touch has had a significant impact on my life. I am the husband of a Moms In Touch mother. My wife has always been loving and devoted to our children, but she would be the first one to

Let's Pray

Below is a list of areas for you to concentrate your prayers on. Pray:

- That the spiritual blindness generated by the Enemy would be lifted from students, teachers, and administrators so they can clearly hear the good news of the Gospel and come to faith in Jesus Christ.
- That Christian students would see their campuses as their mission fields, looking for opportunities to share their faith.
- That our schools will be directed by biblical values and high moral standards.
- That the parachurch organizations and youth pastors on the campuses would not grow weary or lose heart but be strengthened by the Holy Spirit to have endurance and patience.
- That students get caught when guilty.
- For a sweeping movement of student-led prayer and Bible clubs on every school campus.
- That the stronghold of drug use, sexual immorality, and violence be broken. Ask God to reveal any other stronghold that needs to come down.
- That God would bring about racial reconciliation among the students.
- That Christian teachers and staff will unite in prayer on their campus.
- That Christian teachers will recognize secular philosophies within the curriculum and openly illustrate the Christian point of view as well.
- That God would raise up Christian educators for all our campuses.
- For your school for protection from violent assault.
- For all traumatized children, that their fear will turn to faith in Jesus; that God will grant them peace of mind.
- For spiritual awakening and revival on every school campus.
- That a spirit of prayer would be poured out upon moms all over the world to gather together to pray for their children and schools.

admit that she has also been a champion worrier. Several months after she joined a MITI group, I began to see God take her worries and fears and replace them with peace of mind and greater faith.

"I wanted to grow in my faith, too. I had been a Christian for years, loved to study the Bible, but I had never had much interest in prayer meetings.

"One night after dinner, my wife and I were in our Jacuzzi, and I asked her, 'I don't know how you pray for a whole hour at MIT, but would you teach me?'

"She suggested we pray right then and that we go through the four steps of prayer. About an hour later, looking a little like prunes, we emerged.

"In the days and weeks that followed, my wife and I prayed together regularly, and I began to get up earlier in the morning to have an extra hour to pray before I did my Bible study. Before I knew it, God had added new joy and excitement to my spiritual life."

Christian Schools Need Prayer Too

Many of the prayers lifted up for public schools can be prayed for Christian schools too. Robin, who has devoted thirteen years to praying for Christian schools, remembers the morning she had her first informational meeting for moms to share her desire to start a prayer group for a Christian elementary school. The first woman who came remarked, "Where are all the moms? I expected to see your street lined with cars—after all, we are a Christian school." She soon learned we can become complacent in our Christian schools. We can think our children are just fine. Why do they need extra prayer? We forget that our children are growing up in a sinful, ungodly world and will face the same challenges and temptations as any other child.

We must keep this vision before us, whether our children are in public or private schools: Children and schools are starving for prayer. The flood of evil that's drowning our land and affecting our children and schools can be restrained. Oswald Chambers wrote, "By intercessory prayer, we can hold off Satan from other lives and give the Holy Ghost a chance with them."[9] I see God pouring out the spirit of prayer on moms all over the world.

Moms' prayers are "something powerful to be reckoned with" (James 5:16, MESSAGE). Moms from every evangelical denomination are rising to the challenge of taking time out of busy schedules to gather together to pray, to be repairers of the breach in the wall. Moms are giving the best gift they possibly can to their children—their prayers.

The Gift of Prayer Around the World

And God is raising up moms from every nation, tongue, and people group. Our sisters in India began touching heaven one evening as they were praying for their children and couldn't stop—they prayed through the night. They were living Isaiah 62:6–7, "I have posted watchmen [intercessors] on your walls, O Jerusalem; they will never be silent day or night. You who call on the LORD, give yourselves no rest, and give him no rest till he establishes Jerusalem and makes her the praise of the earth." These women couldn't rest until they prayed all that God had placed on their hearts.

Sharon Arrington shares how she experienced moms pouring out their hearts like water—literally. When presenting MITI in Uganda, she taught the mothers how to pray Scripture prayers for their children. The women fell to their knees and sobbed for their children, leaving little pools of tears on the ground.

A mother in Egypt says, "We cry for our children every day because they go to their schools, not being taught a thing about Christ. We are in a state of despair. But thanks be to God who sent you to us with a new vision. We've begun to gather sisters to pray for our children, our schools, and the teachers. Now we are no longer hopeless; now we know what we should do for the sake of our children and their schools."

Olga de Tamacas, who lives in El Salvador, reports, "Mothers in our country, in addition to all the problems shared by moms around the world, are facing the effects of a twelve-year civil war. Our youth are violent, and firearms are common in our society. All this, added to family disintegration, has brought two scourges that have plunged our nation into despair: youth gangs and kidnapping. But Moms In

Touch gave new hope to Salvadoran mothers. Everywhere the idea of praying for children in our schools is presented, moms tell us, 'This is what we needed. How come nobody thought of it before?'"

Colleen Reph, who is on the Washington State MITI team, visited women in Russia and later said, "One of the most wonderful things about sharing with the moms in Russia is that, although our language isn't the same and we can't communicate word to word very well, they would come up to me at the end of our meetings and put their hands over my heart and on their hearts to tell me that they understood, wanting me to know that our hearts are the same. Moms' hearts are the same for our children around the world."

Unique Prayer Groups
Moms in Prison Pray

Women in prison long to pray for their children too. MITI groups meet in more than ten prisons.

Martha was sent to prison for embezzling money from the company she worked for. Just before she was sentenced, she rededicated her life to the Lord. For her, one of the hardships of being imprisoned was not being able to care for and protect her children. Finding out that 75 percent of the seven hundred prisoners were moms and wanting to be close to her own children, Martha decided to start a prison MITI group. "At the first meeting we had fifteen moms," Martha said, "and we covered forty-five kids and twenty schools in prayer. When the Lord called me to lead MITI in prison, I was scared. I was afraid of persecution from other inmates and from the prison staff. Instead, MITI enabled me to develop friendships with moms. As a prisoner, nothing—not driving my kids to soccer games, doing their laundry, washing their dishes, or any other daily 'mom' duties—interferes with the most important duty, praying for my children."

Home-Schooling Moms Pray

Home-schooling moms are seeing the need to unite in prayer. They have a unique situation as they have the dual roles of teacher and mom. One home-schooling mom expresses her love for MITI because of her need for support and prayers. She says, "We love praying for the teachers, because we get to pray for ourselves. And we get to pray for our husbands because they are the principals. Our whole family is prayed for in the MITI hour. How neat is that!"

Grandmothers Pray

In this day and age when our families seem to be scattered to the far corners of the earth, one way to feel close to loved ones is through prayer. This is especially true for grandmothers. On the rise are our Grandmothers In Touch groups. Grandmas are having meaningful regular contact with their grandchildren, asking the children how they can pray for them, for their teachers, friends, and schools. Through answered prayer these grandmothers are teaching their grandchildren that a loving God cares about them.

Watch out next generation—grandmas are praying!

Moms in the Work Force Pray

Mothers who work full-time outside their homes have a great burden to pray for their children. Many times they feel out of touch. Being in a Working Moms In Touch group helps them keep in closer contact with the schools and their kids because of prayer.

One working mom wrote me to share the wonderful support she had from four other working moms who prayed with her. They meet every Saturday at 5:30 A.M. in the basement of a bank where one of the moms works. She said they "come as they are"—some in bathrobes and slippers.

Tragedies Call Moms to Pray

Women who are a part of MITI around the country and the world join in prayer for tragedies that occur with our children and schools. This powerful network of praying moms immediately go to prayer on another's behalf.

That network was evidenced when the tragic news about the shooting at Columbine High School in Littleton, Colorado, was released. Two young gunmen had killed twelve fellow students, a teacher, and finally, themselves.

One of the children shot was John Tomlin, the son of Doreen, a MITI mom. Alisa, the MITI leader for Columbine, said, "The outpouring of love from MITI women around the world was overwhelming. We received hundreds and hundreds of letters and gifts for the Tomlins and the other families. Doreen expressed to me that she read the letters from the MITI ladies over and over again. They spoke the truth to her and reaffirmed her faith that God was in control."

Doreen says, "I prayed for protection for our children; yet, as it was pointed out to me, if all 1,800 kids had died as the gunmen intended, the Christian kids' testimonies might have been drowned out. It's healing to see someone come to Christ because of John's death. John's best friend said yes to Jesus after John died. This young man was one of many who accepted Christ."

Alisa adds: "We had prayed that Columbine would be a light to the rest of the world. God answered our prayers in greater ways than we could have imagined. I have never seen God working so visibly. It's been more than we can absorb. So much joy together with incredible grief. What Satan meant for destruction, God has restored a hundredfold. Instead of losing children at that school, the Lord has increased His flock. My message to moms is keep praying. He is there."

Nothing can prepare you to receive news of the sudden death of your child. What a privilege and honor to stand in the gap for those whom God has allowed to go through such pain.

Thanks Mom

The children catch the vision of what it means to have their moms pray for them, including my daughter, Trisha. "When I think about the women who meet to pray for their kids every week, all around the world, I feel emotions that run deep. I'm grateful for the women who have bathed my life in prayer for so many years. I know for a fact that I wouldn't be where I am right now if they hadn't lifted me up in prayer. I've experienced firsthand the giving heart of a mother, and I will be forever blessed by her consistency to do what she does best—pray."

Not every child can verbalize what Trisha has, but I extend to each mom the thanks her child would give if he or she could.

For all moms who pray:

Thank You Mom

Thank you, thank you for all the times
You pray for me each week
For sacrificing that special hour
With other moms who seek.

Who seek God's will in their child's life
And know this is the way
To share their hearts with the Creator
So we can grow holy each day.

You'll never know how much it means
When you cover me in prayer.
It brings a warmth within my heart
To feel how much you care.

Don't ever stop praying for me, dear Mom,
Your seeds of love will be
The way I'll learn to love this God
You are praying to for me.

Cathy Roby

Isaiah's prayer for Jerusalem helps me to verbalize a prayer to God for our children and schools. Will you pray with me?

> **Almighty God, because we love our children, because our hearts yearn for their schools, we cannot remain silent. We will not stop praying until their righteousness shines like the dawn, and their salvation blazes like a burning torch. May they be called the Holy People and the People Redeemed by the Lord. And may their schools be known as the Desirable Place and the City No Longer Forsaken (Isaiah 62:1, 12). In Jesus' name, amen.**

12. *Keep Praying No Matter What!*

Lynne wondered if she would ever see a change in her daughter's unhappy life. She says, "Julie was one of those rebellious teenagers who couldn't be told anything but had to experience all the bad things for herself. My prayer group prevailed in prayer for her through the years of her depression, self-mutilation, and suicide attempts. My prayer partners didn't even give up when three days after her eighteenth birthday she married a man, who one week later began an affair and then physically abused her.

"Ten months after she married, she divorced her husband and went back to the college she had dropped out of to marry him. That was a huge answer to prayer because it took a lot of courage to return to a setting where all the kids knew what had happened.

"Then Julie was invited on a weekend camping trip with about fifteen other students. But she decided not to go when she found out they were planning to get drunk and high. My prayer group then asked God to stop the students from going on the trip.

"Julie called me the day of the trip. 'Mom, it's raining so hard I can't even see across the parking lot to the next dorm.' I said, 'Did the other kids go camping?' 'Of course not. It's been pouring all day.' I then told her our group had prayed the Lord would keep them from making the trip. She was quiet for a minute and then asked, 'Do you mean you all can pray and make it rain?' Needless to say, I got quite a laugh out of that.

"After years of running from the Lord, Julie finally surrendered her life to God. She dropped by the house as our prayer group was starting to pray. I told her I was sorry I couldn't talk to her right then. She said, 'Mother, did you tell those moms they saved my life?' 'Yes, Julie, I did.'"

God says, "Those who hope in me will not be disappointed" (Isaiah 49:23). What a wonderful promise for moms who carry heavy burdens for their children. We are even told by Paul in Romans 12:12 to be "joyful in hope," for "faith is being sure of what we hope for and certain of what we do not see" (Hebrews 11:1).

Prevailing Prayer

During life's storms, when our children aren't walking with the Lord, or when a debilitating illness persists, or when a husband loses his job, we cling to God's words by faith. His words are our lifeline, and prayer is our lifeboat.

What is prevailing prayer? Prevailing prayer is persistent prayer. It's devoting ourselves to stay the course until the answer comes (Colossians 4:2). It's believing that our prayers will transform other's lives. It's tiptoe anticipation, just waiting for the God of heaven and earth to burst forth with the answer.

> *Prevailing prayer is tiptoe anticipation, just waiting for the God of heaven and earth to burst forth with the answer.*

And prevailing prayer is the wrestling kind of prayer that Jacob engaged in with the angel in Genesis 32:24. He wrestled, he wept, and he prayed (Hosea 12:4). His faith wasn't shaken, even though the blessing was detained. He wrestled not in his own strength, nor did he prevail in his own strength but God's strength.

Consider the following encouragements to prevail in prayer.

> Will he plead against me with great power? No, but he would put strength in me. (Job 23:6, KJV)
>
> [It's] not by might nor by power, but by my Spirit, says the LORD Almighty. (Zechariah 4:6)

> In the same way, the Spirit helps us in our weakness. We do not know what we ought to pray for, but the Spirit himself intercedes for us with groans that words cannot express. (Romans 8:26)

That's how we pray for our children! Hold on fervently, earnestly, passionately, intensely, vehemently. Like Jacob, we can decide to not let go until God blesses our child—until He answers. By God's strength we will prevail. "Lord, I will not leave You unless You bless my children." Prayer like that is born out of passion for God; He is our only hope.

What heart issues do you need to prevail in prayer about?

Prevailing prayer is hanging on to God's promises until the answer comes, no matter how long it takes. As Gary Bergel, president of Intercessors for America, says, we pray "until He settles, resolves, finishes or initiates a Kingdom solution to an appointed matter."[1] A prevailing intercessor trusts God's timing for the answer. She knows that with God a thousand years are like a day (Psalm 90:4).

One mom decided her child's school needed a group to pray for it, but despite placing information about forming a group in the newspaper and making announcements at church, no other mom came to join her. Each week, this mom faithfully set up chairs in the meeting room and then proceeded to pray by herself for an hour. And each week her daughter would ask her, "Did anyone come to pray with you?" The mom answered, "Jesus sat in one of those chairs." After four years of being a one-mom group, she finally was joined by twelve other women.

Let's take seriously Jesus' command: "They ought always to pray and not to turn coward—faint, lose heart and give up" (Luke 18:1, AMP). Persevering prayer brings us closer to God. We need the comfort of His voice, the reassurance of His presence. That's what my husband's favorite verse says to us. "But those who hope in the LORD will renew their strength. They will soar on wings like eagles; they will run and not grow weary, they will walk and not be faint" (Isaiah 40:31).

God's Part, Our Part

As I was reading Jean Fleming's book, *A Mother's Heart*, in which she recounted a story from 2 Kings, I realized how suited that story was to praying. It reminded me that, while we can do some things, other things only God can do.

Three kings joined forces to fight against the Moabites. As these armies were chasing the enemy, they found themselves in the middle of the desert without water. They and their animals were dying of thirst. Elisha the prophet was sent to inquire of the Lord what to do.

Elisha said, "This is what the LORD says: Make this valley full of ditches. For this is what the LORD says: You will see neither wind nor rain, yet this valley will be filled with water, and you, your cattle and your other animals will drink. This is an easy thing in the eyes of the LORD" (2 Kings 3:16–18).

If the people wanted water, they had to dig the ditches. Their tongues were sticking to the roofs of their mouths, their lips were parched, and their brows were sweaty. All of them were weary, some probably fainted as they worked. But to witness the miracle, they had to do their part.

> *We must settle in our hearts that, no matter what, our Lord tells us to keep praying— right up to the end.*

How long and how deep were those ditches? We don't know. What we do know is "the next morning, about the time for offering the sacrifice, there it was—water flowing from the direction of Edom. And the land was filled with water" (verse 20).

We must settle in our hearts that, no matter what, our Lord tells us to keep praying—right up to the end. First Peter 4:7 says, "The end of the world is coming soon. Therefore, be earnest and disciplined in your prayers" (NLT). When God comes back to Earth, He wants to find His bride praying.

Sometimes do you feel hopeless, that your faith is weak, and that your strength is depleted? Jesus says, even then, keep talking to Him. Yes, even if you have lost heart. No one understands like Jesus. "For we do not have a high priest who is unable to sympathize with our weaknesses, but we have one who has been tempted in every way, just as we are—yet was without sin. Let us then approach the throne of grace with confidence, so that we may receive mercy and find grace to help us in our time of need" (Hebrews 4:15–16).

You could have the privilege of going to Jesus on behalf of a dear friend who is suffering from a long-term illness such as multiple sclerosis. While you could pray for her healing, you might also pray that God will give her the grace to endure her cross, that her inner being would be strengthened with Holy Spirit power, that she would see her Savior in ways she has never seen Him before, and that she understands and knows how wide, long, and deep Jesus' love is for her. But most importantly, whatever you pray for her, prevail in your prayers, don't stop.

You can also prevail in prayer for people whose lives brush against yours for a brief time. For example, I'm praying for a young woman my daughter-in-love met in the doctor's waiting room. This girl was all alone, eight months pregnant, and with cancer in her uterus. The doctors want her to abort her baby. I pray for her salvation and that God would bring people into her life to love her and to help. That the Prince of Peace would be at home in her heart.

So many situations require prevailing prayer. These people need others who will cry out day and night to God. As Isaiah 62:6 says, "I have posted watchmen on your walls, O Jerusalem; they will never be silent day or night. You who call on the LORD, give yourselves no rest."

A God Eager to Help

Not praying because we aren't sure what to pray isn't the right choice. We must trust the Holy Spirit to interpret our fumbling thoughts perfectly before the Father. If we only understood how much God wants to help.

Spurgeon writes what he envisions as God's response when we pray.

It is but a small thing for Me, your God, to help you. Consider what I have done already. What! Not help you? Why, I bought you with My blood. What! Not help you? I have died for you; and if I have done that greater, will I not do the less? Help you! It is the least thing I will ever do for you; I have done more, and will do more. Before the world began, I chose you. I made the covenant for you; I laid aside My glory and became a man for you; I gave My life for you; and if I did all this, I will surely help you now. In helping you, I am giving you what I have bought for you already. If you had need of a thousand times as much help, I would give it to you; you require little compared with what I am ready to give. 'Tis much for you to need, but it is nothing for me to bestow.[2]

How can we not trust a God like that?

One day I was driving through a long stretch of road with grain fields on both sides. I happened to see one lone tree way off in the distance. It was leaning at a forty-five degree angle. Day after day, year after year, the tree slowly had succumbed to the prevailing winds that blew across the plain.

Our prevailing prayers are like the wind of the Holy Spirit, causing the object of our prayer to bend before its persistent force. On any given day we may not see the effects of our prayers; nonetheless, God is at work.

Let's Pray

Praying for long-term, not-easily-resolved issues tries our patience, our faith, and our creativity. After awhile it's hard to know what to pray. Using Scripture for your prayers helps you to persevere. In the following scriptural prayers you can insert the person's name into the blanks. Know that God promises you that His Word will not return empty. No matter how long it takes for the answer to come, Jesus encourages you to "always pray and not give up" (Luke 18:1).

For Prodigals

Gracious Father, reach down your hand from on high and deliver _____ and rescue him from the mighty waters, from the hands of foreigners whose mouths are full of lies, whose right hands are deceitful. (Psalm 144:7–8)

For Husbands

*My faithful Father, I pray that you will give _____
an undivided heart and put a new spirit in him; please
remove from _____ a heart of stone and give him a
heart of flesh. Then _____ will follow your decrees
and will be careful to keep your laws. May _____ know
that you are his God. (Ezekiel 11:19–20)*

For Long-term Illness

*Dear merciful Lord, I ask that you would strengthen
_____ according to your glorious might so that _____
may have great endurance and patience. (Colossians 1:11)*

For Salvation

*Loving Father, I ask that you would open
_____'s eyes and turn him from darkness to light,
and from the power of Satan to God, so that he might
receive forgiveness of sins and a place among those who
are sanctified by faith. (Acts 26:18)*

For Anxieties

*Heavenly Father, I pray in Jesus' name that
_____ would not be anxious or fret about anything, but that in everything, he would through prayer
and petition with thanksgiving, present his requests to
you. Thank you for the promise, that you will grant to
_____ your peace that transcends all understanding, and that you will guard his heart and mind
in Christ Jesus. (Philippians 4:6–7)*

A Time for Action, a Time for Prayer

But sometimes we have trouble waiting for the answer. Instead of
trusting, we step in and take matters in our own hands. When we do,
we run the risk of stepping in where God may have intended something altogether different. Before we act, we need to ask God what He
wants us to do—or to refrain from doing.

We're like the little boy who found a cocoon. He sat for a while and watched the butterfly struggle to force its body through a small hole. The boy thought it was sad that the butterfly had to work so hard with seemingly little results. So he decided to help. Taking a pair of scissors, he snipped the strands of the cocoon that still held the butterfly imprisoned. The cocoon fell open and out crawled the butterfly. But its body was swollen and had small, shriveled wings. It never could fly. What the boy didn't understand was that the intense struggle to break free was needed to initiate circulation in its wings.

Many of our children struggle to find their own faith. Our job is to love them unconditionally and prevail in prayer. As we seek God, we must ask Him to give us the wisdom to know when to step in and when to keep silent. I know this isn't easy. But rest assured that your loving God is right there with you, scooping up your hurting puddle of a heart and carrying you close to His heart. As Scripture says, "And the one the LORD loves rests between his shoulders" (Deuteronomy 33:12).

Oh, moms, isn't that wonderful? If we do our work—the work of prayer—if we persevere, digging the ditch, one great day water will appear—the answer to prayer. The miracle isn't hard for God.

On his radio program, Ron Hutchcraft gives hurting parents hope as he reminds them of the story found in Luke 7.

> As Jesus approached the gate of a town called Nain, "a dead person was being carried out—the only son of his mother, and she was a widow. And a large crowd from the town was with her. When the Lord saw her, His heart went to her and He said, 'Don't cry.' Then He went up and touched the coffin and those carrying it stood still. He said, 'Young man, I say to you, get up!' The dead man sat up and began to talk, and Jesus gave him back to his mother."
>
> If Jesus can raise a child from the dead to return him to his mother, don't you think He can bring your son or daughter back from wherever they have wandered? Jesus is calling out to you this very day to say, "Don't give up. Don't lose hope. I've heard your prayers. I'm after him. I'm after her."[3]

Hope is restored when others pray with you. Something wonderful happens when many are praying and tenaciously holding on to the one being prayed for.

The Cumulative Effect

"Our prayers have an accumulative effect," says author Wesley Duewel. "When a dam is erected in a mountain valley, its construction may take many months. Then the water begins accumulating behind the dam, which can take months or even a year or longer. But when the water level reaches the right height, the sluice gates are opened, water begins to turn the generators, and there is tremendous power."

Duewel likens this illustration to persistent, one-accord prayer. "As more and more people unite in prayer or as the prevailing person prays on and on, it seems as if a great mass of prayer is accumulated until suddenly there is a breakthrough and God's will is accomplished. . . . Prayers prayed in the will of God are never lost but are stored until God gives the answer."[4]

The person standing on the dry side of the dam can't see the water accumulating. Then, when that last drop brings the water to the right level, all power breaks lose. Often we stand on the dry side, praying faithfully for a breakthrough in a child's life or our husband's job or our church's disunity or our school being a lighthouse for Jesus. And seemingly nothing happens. But God has heard every prayer, and at His appointed time, all of His power breaks lose.

"I remember literally shaking my fist at God," Jan says as she recounts her prayers for her son, Luke. "He sent me the wrong kid. I wasn't supposed to have a teenager like this—angry, defiant, sneaky, worldly. I had plans to be the world's best mom; how could I have this impossible son?

"As a child, Luke was a joyous, exuberant son but challenging, always pushing. I took comfort in his strong will, thinking he would be strong in resisting peer pressure. Little did I know that most children who are labeled 'strong-willed' actually are *self*-willed, and a self-centered, self-conscious adolescent doesn't want to be different. That was Luke. Living for self and independence, ignoring curfews and courtesies, taking up cigarettes and marijuana, pushing the patience of teachers and parents to the limit.

"I have prayed for Luke all his life, but I'm so grateful that when he was in the third grade, God brought in reinforcements—Moms In Touch. From age eight, those other moms agreed with me before the Father on behalf of my son, had faith when mine was weak, loved him through prayer.

"In our prayer group we pray a bold prayer: that our children will be caught when guilty. I thought many of our prayers fell on God's deaf ears, but *that* prayer God answered over and over again. Luke often was caught in his illegal actions.

"He decided not to go to college after high school. After all, he knew everything. Besides, he would be a multimillionaire with his rock band before long; so a college degree wouldn't be necessary.

"Luke moved out on his own. Then, little by little, we saw glimpses of the invisible work God had been doing all along. Achieving the independence he had craved since birth caused Luke's relationship with us to improve. He asked his dad's advice, chatted about the Dodgers, and had real conversations with me.

"Little-by-little gave way to big-by-big. Luke devoured the Bible, attended church, and gave up bad habits. Since high school, every penny he made, all his hopes, dreams, goals, and time had centered around his band. The band members could scarcely wait to turn twenty-one so they could get gigs in bars and hit the big time. The day came, the gigs came, they were well received. Then God told Luke He wanted to do a new thing.

"This son of ours, who rarely had shared a personal thought or struggle since boyhood, asked his mom and dad to pray as he went to tell the band it was over. The band that played his original songs and for which he was the lead singer. Now, he was going to dash the other members' hopes and years of work because they 'weren't on the same page.'

"Now God has placed new songs on his lips, songs that bring glory to Him. He has emboldened the faith of moms in our group who are still waiting to see their sons and daughters turn wholeheartedly back to God."

Storming the Gates

I'm a mother just like Jan, just like you. I love my children just like you. I pray for them just like you. And, like so many mothers, I have travailed, wept, and stormed the gates of hell for the life of my prodigal.

At times I came before the Lord sobbing for his very life. Then feelings of unworthiness and failure as a mom would slip into my heart. The "if onlys" flooded my mind. How could God use me in ministry when my own family was struggling? How could I tell other moms that God would answer their prayers when I didn't see mine being answered? What would the women think when they heard about my son?

I needed God's strength, wisdom, unfailing love, and courage just to go about my normal activities as a wife, mother, and ministry leader. When I look back on those days, I can only say God's grace—His marvelous, matchless, wonderful grace—sustained me and kept me hoping and functioning.

I remember one day in particular I was feeling unworthy. Then I read Matthew 10:37–38: "Anyone who loves his father or mother more than me is not worthy of me; anyone who loves his son or daughter more than me is not worthy of me; and anyone who does not take his cross and follow me is not worthy of me."

The Holy Spirit stopped me on the phrase, "anyone who does not take his cross and follow me is not worthy of me." My only concern should be carrying my cross, being faithful to what God had called me to do. Even if it was hard. Even if I didn't understand. Even if I felt I couldn't go on.

I prayed, "Oh, Lord, I do love You more than my children, and I want to serve You until You take me home to dwell with You forever. You're right. I can't carry my children's crosses. You will help them to carry theirs, just as You're helping me. What a relief to know that

I'm only responsible for the cross that You have given me. That's all You ask of me. May I be found faithful."

I admire Billy Graham and his wife, Ruth, for being vulnerable concerning their prodigal son, Franklin. They diligently prayed for him and yet continued to serve the Lord. Billy Graham kept preaching in spite of his son's waywardness. Think of the thousands of people who might not have accepted Christ if Reverend Graham had quit preaching the gospel until his son got right with Jesus.

Persevering While Running

Like the Grahams, my task was to persevere in prayer for my children. With joy, I must run with perseverance the race God has marked out for me (Hebrews 12:1–2).

The following thoughts from *Streams in the Desert* ministered greatly to me as I tried to run the race with patience and to serve the Lord while grieving over my child.

> We commonly associate patience with laying down. We think of it as the angel that guards the couch of the invalid. Yet, I do not think the invalid's patience the hardest to achieve. There is a patience which I believe to be harder.... It is the power to *work* under a stroke; to have a great weight at your heart and still to run; to have a deep anguish in your spirit and still perform the daily task.... We are called to bury our sorrows not in lethargic quiescence, but in active service.... There is no burial of sorrow so difficult as that; it is the "*running* with patience."[5]

My children are now adults who each love the Lord. I can declare with John, "I have no greater joy than to hear that my children are walking in the truth" (3 John 4). How I praise God for helping me to keep to the task He had called me to. I would have missed out on so many blessings.

Evelyn Christenson, in her book *What Happens When Women Pray*, says, "Changes take place not when we study about prayer, not when we talk about it, not even when we memorize beautiful Scripture verses on prayer. It is when *we actually pray* that things begin to happen."[6]

That's been my desire throughout this book: to spur you on to greater prayer efforts. For we each have been given the privilege and the responsibility to pray for our loved ones, especially our children. Our prayer legacy is the richest inheritance we could give them. Praying is powerful.

As we've discussed together, because we are God's children, we have certain rights and privileges. We have the authority to come to our heavenly Father on behalf of ourselves and others. God asks us to persevere in our prayers and to pray with confidence. And our Father longs for us to come to His table on a regular basis to communicate with Him. He asks us to bring our hearts, which are a mixture of hope and longing, to Him, asking Him to act on behalf of ourselves and our loved ones. And He's given us the tools to do so with assurances that He longs to respond. That's part of the reason we study Scripture—to know His will and His promises, that we might pray according to them. That's why we pray together— because He has told us power resides in one-accord praying. That's why we enter into the spiritual fray against the darkness as we pray— because He has assured us He will prevail. And that's why we pray for the locale that so profoundly influences our children, their schools. We know God wants them to be spiritually and morally uplifting places. And that's why we pray the four, life-changing prayers—because they help us to focus on each aspect of our relationship with God, praising Him, confessing to Him, thanking Him, and interceding for others before Him.

Now that you've walked through the four steps of prayer for yourself, I hope you've found those steps as exhilarating and worshipful as I do. After using them for twenty years, every time I employ them, I still anticipate discovering a deeper knowledge of God through each step. I've found that each of the four points of prayer is worship, reminding me of God's character and faithfulness—which I've seen expressed time after time. My heart's cry still is, "Lord, teach me to pray." I'm learning to sing my song, just as you are.

So, my dear reader, I pray that singing your song to God is a joy and a blessing—to you and to your Lord. May your notes be high and may you hold them long.

> *Dear loving Father, I pray that the reader would experience Psalm 25:14 (AMP): "The secret [of the sweet, satisfying companionship] of the Lord have they who fear—revere and worship—Him, and He will show them His covenant, and reveal to them its [deep, inner] meaning."*
>
> *Father, may Your words dwell richly in her. May she thirst for You as the deer pants for water. Help her each day to have quiet times with You. Give her assurance that You hear her cries and answer her prayers. May she know the joy of gathering with others to help carry her burdens through prayer. Bless her. Give her the courage, faith, and hope to continue steadfast in prayer—for every child needs a praying mom. Amen and amen.*

Acknowledgments

This book is a miracle of God's grace in my life. I can't remember a day during the writing process that I didn't come before the Lord, crying out, "Lord Jesus, I need Your help. Fill me with Your Holy Spirit so that I might write what is on Your heart." To Him, first and foremost, I give all the honor and glory and praise.

My heartfelt thanks to the staff at Zondervan, especially to Carolyn Blauwkamp, who caught the vision for Moms In Touch International and who first spoke to me about book publishing; to Cindy Hays Lambert, my wonderfully perceptive editor; and to Sue Brower, who, as marketing director, has been a strong supporter of the book from the beginning. To each person at Zondervan, your enthusiasm and belief that God wanted the vision of Moms In Touch International shared through the written word still leaves me breathless and grateful.

My dear agent, Ann Spangler, how lovingly and patiently you encouraged and helped me, especially in the project's beginning stages. Can you believe God put the idea of my writing this book on your heart more than ten years ago! God used you, Ann, in priceless ways you will never know.

Janet Kobobel Grant, I marvel at your editing skills, keen insights, and organizational talents. You always seemed to say just the right words during our weekly chats, giving me the courage to continue. God chose you as my coach for this book. Your "touches" made this book come alive.

For my Moms In Touch Book Intercessor Team (MITI board, state coordinators, regional directors, MITI headquarters staff, MITI friends, and my immediate and extended family), I give God great thanksgiving. You were my inspiration. This book couldn't have been completed without your sacrificial prayers. Thank you for the hours of believing prayer that you prayed for Janet and me. This is truly "our" book.

I especially want to thank Cheri Fuller, Pam Farrel, Marlae Gritter, Charlene Martin, Joanne Harris, and Connie Kennemer for your encouraging notes, phone calls, and emails. They were treasured.

To my wonderful headquarters staff, words can't convey how much I love you and how grateful I am for your faith in me and for your precious prayers on my behalf. I especially want to thank Kathy Gayheart, Julie van der Schalie, Shari Larson, Elaine Minton, and Melanie Collier for your hands of help and for your insights that made the rough places smooth.

I'm thankful to my Thursday noon College Moms In Touch group for your commitment to pray for me each week. I'm grateful to you, Lynne Bechard and Kathleen Wendeln, for keeping my specific prayer requests before the moms. What a joy and delight it has been for me to pray with you.

To the MITI women in the United States and around the world, thank you for sharing your prayer testimonies. Through your vulnerability you have given hope that God does hear and answer prayers to countless others.

And to my family, your prayers and undying faith in me that I "can do all things through Christ who gives me strength" were my source of joy and perseverance. I love you "way past heaven"!

Appendix:
Prayer Lists and Prayer Sheets

Praise: God's Attributes

Shout with joy to God, all the earth! Sing the glory of his name; make his praise glorious!

Psalm 66:1–2

Below is a list of God's attributes, along with Scripture describing each, which you can pray back to God. Definitions are provided for you to consider the various aspects of each attribute and to add depth to the praises you offer to our God.

God Is Supreme

Highest in rank, power, authority; superior, highest in degree; utmost

Genesis 14:19	Acts 17:24–28
Job 11:7–9	Jude 24–25
Isaiah 44:6–8	Nehemiah 9:6
Hebrews 1:4, 6	Psalm 135:5
Deuteronomy 10:14–17	Colossians 1:15–18
Psalm 95:3–7	Revelation 4:8

God Is Sovereign

Holding the position of ruler, royal, reigning; independent of all others; above or superior to all others; controls everything, can do anything

1 Samuel 2:6–8	Psalm 93
Job 42:2	Isaiah 46:9–10

1 Chronicles 29:10–13

Psalm 33:10–11

Psalm 135:6–7

Matthew 10:29–30

2 Chronicles 20:6

Psalm 47:2–3, 7–8

Isaiah 40:10

Romans 8:28

God Is Omnipotent

All powerful; having unlimited power or authority; almighty

2 Chronicles 32:7–8

Psalm 147:5

Habakkuk 3:4

Ephesians 3:20

Psalm 62:11

Isaiah 40:28–31

Matthew 19:26

Colossians 1:10–12

Psalm 89:8–13

Jeremiah 32:17

Ephesians 1:19–20

Hebrews 1:3

God Is Omniscient

Having infinite knowledge; knowing all things

Psalm 44:21

Psalm 147:5

Matthew 6:8

Romans 11:33–34

Psalm 139:1–6

Isaiah 65:24

Matthew 10:30

Colossians 2:3

Psalm 142:3

Daniel 2:22

John 6:64

Hebrews 4:13

God Is Omnipresent

Present in all places at all times

1 Kings 8:27

Psalm 139:5–12

Matthew 28:20

Colossians 1:17

Psalm 31:20

Isaiah 66:1

Acts 17:27–28

2 Timothy 4:16–18

Psalm 46:1–7

Jeremiah 23:24

Romans 8:35, 38–39

Hebrews 13:5

God Is Immutable

Never changing or varying; unchangeable

Numbers 23:19

Psalm 100:5

Isaiah 40:6–8

Hebrews 6:17–19

1 Samuel 15:29

Psalm 102:25–27

Isaiah 51:6

Hebrews 13:8

Psalm 33:11

Psalm 119:89, 152

Malachi 3:6

James 1:17

God Is Faithful

Constant, loyal, reliable, steadfast, unwavering, devoted, true, dependable

Deuteronomy 7:9

Psalm 119:90

Lamentations 3:21–24

2 Timothy 2:13

Psalm 33:4

Psalm 145:13

1 Corinthians 10:13

1 John 1:9

Psalm 89:8

Psalm 146:5–8

2 Timothy 1:12

Revelation 19:11

God Is Holy

Spiritually perfect or pure; sinless; deserving awe, reverence, adoration

Exodus 15:11

Psalm 99

Isaiah 57:15–16

1 Peter 1:15–16

1 Samuel 2:2

Psalm 111:9

Luke 1:49

Revelation 4:8

Psalm 77:13

Isaiah 5:16

Acts 3:13–15

Revelation 15:4

God Is Just

Right or fair, impartial, upright, lawful, correct, true; righteous

Deuteronomy 32:4

Psalm 89:14–16

Isaiah 30:18

Romans 3:25–26

2 Chronicles 19:7
Psalm 119:137–138
Zephaniah 3:5
2 Thessalonians 1:5–7

Psalm 9:7–10
Psalm 145:17
John 5:30
Revelation 15:3–4

God Is Wise

From the root *to know* or *to see*, but wisdom goes past knowledge to understanding and action; having keen perception, discernment; power of judging rightly; always making right choices

1 Chronicles 28:9
Proverbs 2:6
Isaiah 55:8–9
Romans 16:27
Psalm 92:5
Proverbs 3:19–20

Daniel 2:20–22
Colossians 2:2–3
Psalm 147:5
Isaiah 28:29
Romans 11:33–34
James 3:17

God Is Eternal

Without beginning or end; existing through all time; everlasting

Exodus 3:14–15
Nehemiah 9:5
Psalm 93:2
Romans 1:20
Exodus 15:18
Psalm 45:6

Isaiah 26:4
1 Timothy 1:17
Deuteronomy 33:27
Psalm 90:1–2
Jeremiah 31:3
Revelation 1:8, 18

God Is the Creator

The one who brought the universe and all matter and life in it into existence

Genesis 1:1
Psalm 104
Jeremiah 10:12
Colossians 1:16
Psalm 95:3–7
Psalm 148:1–6

John 1:3
Hebrews 1:2
Psalm 100:3
Isaiah 42:5
Acts 17:24–28
Revelation 10:6

God Is Good

Virtuous, excellent; upright; essentially, absolutely, and consummately good

Psalm 25:8

Psalm 119:68

Jeremiah 33:11

John 10:11

Psalm 34:8

Psalm 136:1

Nahum 1:7

1 Timothy 4:4

Psalm 86:5

Psalm 145:9

Mark 10:18

2 Peter 1:3–4

Quiet Time—Praise

I will praise you, O Lord my God, with all my heart; I will glorify your name forever.

Psalm 86:12

The following provides you with a way to direct your thoughts as you praise God. This simple method of journaling can become a record of your prayer times.

Date: _____ Attribute: _____

Definition:

Scripture:

Thoughts/Prayer:

Date: _____ Attribute: _____

Definition:

Scripture:

Thoughts/Prayer:

Date: _____ Attribute: _____

Definition:

Scripture:

Thoughts/Prayer:

Date: _____ Attribute: _____

Definition:

Scripture:

Thoughts/Prayer:

Confession Helps

Anyone, then, who knows the good he ought to do and doesn't do it, sins.

James 4:17

The following list compiled by Evelyn Christenson may be used as a tool for confession.[1] It will help to get you started in thinking about areas that need confession. Every "yes" answer to a question represents a sin that needs to be confessed.

In everything give thanks, for this is the will of God in Christ Jesus concerning you.

1 Thessalonians 5:18, KJV

Do you worry about anything? Have you failed to thank God for *all* things, the seemingly bad as well as the good? Do you neglect to give thanks at mealtime?

Now unto him who is able to do exceeding abundantly above all that we ask or think, according to the power that worketh in us.

Ephesians 3:20, KJV

Do you fail to attempt things for God because you are not talented enough? Do feelings of inferiority keep you from trying to serve God? When you do accomplish something for Christ, do you fail to give Him all the glory?

But ye shall receive power, after the Holy Spirit is come upon you: and ye shall be witnesses unto me both in Jerusalem, and in all Judea, and in Samaria, and unto the uttermost part of the earth.

Acts 1:8, KJV

Have you failed to be a witness with your life for Christ? Have you felt it was enough just to live your Christianity and not to witness with your mouth to the lost?

For I say ... to every man that is among you, not to think of himself more highly than he ought to think.

Romans 12:3, KJV

Are you proud of *your* accomplishments, *your* talents, *your* family? Do you fail to see others as better than yourself, more important than yourself in the body of Christ? Do you insist on your own rights? Do you think as a Christian you are doing quite well? Do you rebel at God wanting to change you?

Let all bitterness, and wrath, and anger, and clamor, and evil speaking be put away from you, with all malice.

Ephesians 4:31, KJV

Do you complain, find fault, argue? Do you have a critical spirit? Do you carry a grudge against Christians of another group because they don't see eye-to-eye with you on all things? Do you speak unkindly about people when they are not present? Are you angry with yourself? Others? God?

What? Know ye not that your body is the temple of the Holy Spirit who is in you, whom ye have of God, and ye are not your own?

1 Corinthians 6:19, KJV

Are you careless with your body? Are you guilty of not caring for it as the temple of the Holy Spirit in eating and exercising? Do you defile your body with unholy sexual acts?

Thanksgiving

To help direct your thinking to those people and circumstances you're thankful for, think about these and then thank God for:

His constant presence with your husband and children
The times He set you free from your fears
The blessings of being part of the body of Christ
The ways He has carried you in difficult times
The ability to serve your family
How He provides for all your needs
His comfort in times of discouragement, weariness, and loneliness

Intercession Day by Day

Sometimes we can feel we have so much to pray about that we become overwhelmed. You might want to focus on a different topic each day. Here are some suggested topics and Scriptures.

Every Day: Your Family
Husband:

Psalm 1:1–3
Isaiah 61:1–3
Psalm 19:7–11
Ezekiel 36:26–27

Psalm 32:7–8
Ephesians 1:17–18
Psalm 92:12–15
2 Thessalonians 1:11–12

Children (see pags 203–204.)

Sunday: Church

For your pastor, elders, Sunday school teachers, missionaries, evangelists, theological schools

2 Corinthians 7:1
Colossians 1:9–11
Ephesians 4:1–3
Colossians 4:3–4

Ephesians 6:19
1 Thessalonians 5:16–22
Philippians 1:9–11
2 Timothy 2:15

Monday: Education

For the superintendent, principal, teachers, professors, staff

Psalm 106:3
Acts 26:18
Proverbs 6:16–19
Colossians 2:8

Proverbs 10:9
1 Timothy 6:20
Proverbs 14:34
Titus 2:7–8

Tuesday: Those in Authority

For the president, vice president, cabinet members, senators, congressmen, local leaders, police officers, firefighters

Deuteronomy 18:9–11
Proverbs 6:16–19
2 Chronicles 19:7
Proverbs 14:34

Psalm 33:12
Philippians 1:9–10
Proverbs 3:5–6
2 Timothy 2:25

Wednesday: Non-believers

Romans 2:4
1 Timothy 2:4–6
Romans 10:1, 13–15
2 Timothy 2:25–26

2 Corinthians 4:3–4
1 Peter 1:18–19
Colossians 1:13
2 Peter 3:9

Thursday: Persecuted Christians

Psalm 79:11
Colossians 4:3
Psalm 80:17–19
2 Thessalonians 3:3, 5

Philippians 1:20
Hebrews 13:20–21
Colossians 1:11
1 Peter 2:15

Friday: Media

For people who work for the newspapers, TV, radio, magazines, movies

2 Chronicles 7:13–14
Ezekiel 18:30–32
Proverbs 1:7
Colossians 2:8

Proverbs 15:28
1 Thessalonians 2:4
Isaiah 1:16–17
1 John 2:15–16

Saturday: Fellow Believers

Proverbs 9:10
Philippians 1:4–6
John 17:17
Philippians 1:9–11

Ephesians 1:16–19
Colossians 4:12
Ephesians 3:14–20
Hebrews 10:24

Quiet Time—Intercession

This is the confidence we have in approaching God: that if we ask anything according to his will, he hears us. And if we know that he hears us—whatever we ask—we know that we have what we asked of him.

1 John 5:14–15

Use these pages to provide a journal for the intercessions you make. As you look back on the answers, your heart will be blessed and strengthened to keep praying.

Date: _____

Scripture Reference: _____

Scripture Request (place name in the Scripture): _____

Specific Request:

Date/Answer: _____

Date: _____

Scripture Reference: _____

Scripture Request (place name in the Scripture): _____

Specific Request:

Date/Answer: _____

Date: _____

Scripture Reference: _____

Scripture Request (place name in the Scripture): _____

Specific Request:

Date/Answer: _____

Date: _____

Scripture Reference: _____

Scripture Request (place name in the Scripture): _____

Specific Request:

Date/Answer: _____

Date: _____

Scripture Reference: _____

Scripture Request (place name in the Scripture): _____

Specific Request:

Date/Answer: _____

Date: _____

Scripture Reference: _____

Scripture Request (place name in the Scripture): _____

Specific Request:

Date/Answer: _____

Date: _____

Scripture Reference: _____

Scripture Request (place name in the Scripture): _____

Specific Request:

Date/Answer: _____

Intercession:
Praying Scripturally for
Our Children

Following are prayers that are Scripture verses you can pray for your child.

Will Be Obedient

Give my son/daughter a good heart toward God, so that he/she will want to obey you in the smallest detail. (1 Chronicles 29:19, TLB*)*

Will Love the Word of God

That my son/daughter would guard (God's) word as his/her most precious possession. That he/she would write them down, and also keep them deep within his/her heart. (Proverbs 7:2–3, TLB*)*

Will Desire to Be with Those Who Love the Lord

That my son/daughter will enjoy the companionship of those who love the Lord and have pure hearts. (2 Timothy 2:22, TLB*)*

Will Know Jesus' Voice and Follow Only Him

That my son/daughter will follow (Jesus), because he/she knows his voice. He/she will never [on any account] follow a stranger, but will run away from him because he/she does not know the voice of strangers or recognize their call. (John 10:4–5, AMP*)*

Will Be Quick to Confess Sin

The high and lofty one who inhabits eternity, the Holy One, says this: I live in that high and holy place where those with contrite, humble spirits dwell; and I refresh the humble and give new courage to those with repentant hearts. (Isaiah 57:15, TLB) May my son/daughter have such a heart.

Will Clearly See the Difference Between Right and Wrong

I pray that my son/daughter will see clearly the difference between right and wrong, and will be inwardly clean, no one being able to criticize him/her from now until our Lord returns. (Philippians 1:10, TLB)

Will Be Safe from Bullies

Hide my son/daughter in the shelter of your presence, safe beneath your hand, safe from all conspiring men. (Psalm 31:20, TLB)

Will Know God Better

I ask that the God of our Lord Jesus Christ, the Father of glory, may give my son/daughter the spirit of wisdom and revelation in the knowledge of him. (Ephesians 1:17)

Will Be Saved

And give one heart—a new heart—and put a new spirit within him/her; and take the stony [unnaturally hardened] heart out of his/her flesh, and give him/her a heart of flesh [sensitive and responsive to the touch of his/her God]. (Ezekiel 11:19, AMP)

Will Be Proud to Be a Christian

That your words are what sustains; they are food to his/her hungry soul. They bring joy to his/her sorrowing heart and delight him/her. How proud he/she is to bear your name, O Lord. (Jeremiah 15:16, TLB)

Notes

Chapter 2: Becoming a Confident Pray–er

1. Warren Myers with Ruth Myers, *How to Be Effective in Prayer* (Colorado Springs: NavPress, 1983), xvii.

2. Ney Bailey letter, November-December 1986.

Chapter 3: Life-Changing Prayer

1. Myers, *How to Be Effective in Prayer,* 8.

2. E. Stanley Jones, *How to Pray* (Reston, Va.: Intercessors for America), 11–12.

Chapter 4: Praise: Praying According to God's Attributes

1. Jack R. Taylor, *The Hallelujah Factor* (Nashville: Broadman, 1983), 25.

2. Dick Eastman, *The Hour That Changes the World* (Grand Rapids, Mich.: Baker, 1978), 23.

3. C. H. Spurgeon, *The Practice of Praise* (New Kensington, Penn.: Whitaker House, 1995), 13.

4. Spurgeon, *The Practice of Praise,* 16–17.

5. Eastman, *The Hour That Changes the World,* 24.

6. Ibid.

7. A. W. Tozer, *The Knowledge of the Holy* (New York: Harper & Row, 1961), 20.

Chapter 5: Confessions: Removing Rubble

1. Eastman, *The Hour That Changes the World,* 43.

2. Jennifer Kennedy Dean, *He Restores My Soul* (Nashville: Broadman & Holman, 1999), 33.

3. Joy Dawson, *Intimate Friendship with God* (Old Tappan, N.J.: Chosen Books, 1986), 57.

4. Alister E. McGrath, ed., *The NIV Thematic Reference Bible* (Grand Rapids, Mich.: Zondervan, 1999), 1058.

5. David Daniels, "Encountering God in the Lord's Prayer," *Discipleship Journal* (May/June 2002), 64.

6. Bill Gothard, *Ten Reasons for Alumni to Be Encouraged* (Oak Brook, Ill.: Institute in Basic Life Principles, 1992), 9.

7. Ron Mehl, *God Works the Night Shift* (Sisters, Ore.: Multnomah Publishers, 1994), 98–100.

Chapter 6: Thanksgiving: The Expression of a Grateful Heart

1. O. Hallesby, *Prayer* (Minneapolis: Augsburg Fortress, 1994).

2. Merlin Carothers, *Power in Praise* (Escondido, Calif.: Merlin R. Carothers, 1972).

3. Mehl, *God Works the Night Shift*, 27, 29–30.

Chapter 7: Intercession: Standing in the Gap

1. Alice Smith, *Beyond the Veil* (Houston, Tex.: SpiriTruth Publishing, 1996), 28.

2. Jennifer Kennedy Dean, "Alternate-Route Prayer," *Pray* (July/August 2002), 16.

3. Eastman, *The Hour That Changes the World*, 76.

4. Andrew Murray, *Prayer: A 31-Day Plan to Enrich Your Prayer Life* (Uhrichsville, Ohio: Barbour, 1995).

5. Mrs. Charles E. Cowman, *Streams in the Desert*, (Grand Rapids, Mich.: Zondervan, 1925).

Chapter 8: Praying According to God's Promises

1. Martin R. De Haan II, *How Does God Keep His Promises?* (Grand Rapids, Mich.: Radio Bible Class, 1989), 4–5.

2. Ibid. 18.

3. Ibid. 11.

4. Ibid. 7.

5. E. M. Bounds, *The Possibilities of Prayer* (Chicago: Moody Press, 1980), chapter 3, page 1.

6. Ron Hutchcraft, "The Store Is Yours," *A Word with You*, #4017, *www.gospelcom.net*.

Chapter 9: One-Accord Praying

1. Ray Stedman, *Talking with the Father* (Grand Rapids, Mich.: Discovery House, 1997), 101.

2. Rosalind Rinker, *Prayer: Conversing with God* (Grand Rapids, Mich.: Zondervan, 1959), 46.

3. Rinker, *Prayer,* 23.

4. Evelyn Christenson, *What Happens When Women Pray* (Wheaton, Ill: Victor, 1980), 40.

Chapter 10: Get Ready for a Fight: Warfare Prayers

1. Tim Sheets, *Armed and Battle Ready* (self-published, 1985), 15–16.

2. Ibid.

3. Charles Stanley, "The Real War," two-tape series.

Chapter 11: Praying for Our Schools

1. National Center for Education website. *http://nces.ed.gov//pubs2002/digest2001/ch1.*

2. "Focus on the Family Features Moms in Touch," *Heart to Heart* newsletter (Spring 2000), 4.

3. *www.syatp.com*

4. CBN news story, Sept. 23, 2002.

5. *www.bibleinschools.org*

6. *www.gtbe.org, Gateways to Better Education* newsletter.

7. Editors of *Religion Today, crosswalk.com,* March 29, 2001.

8. Personal correspondence, 2002.

9. Oswald Chambers, *My Utmost for His Highest* (Uhrichsville, Ohio: Barbour, 1998).

Chapter 12: Keep Praying No Matter What!

1. Gary Bergel, "A Time for Prevailing Prayer," *Intercessors for America Newsletter,* Feb. 2001, 2.

2. Charles H. Spurgeon, *Morning and Evening* (Grand Rapids, Mich.: Zondervan, 1980), Morning, Jan. 15.

3. Ron Hutchcraft, "Child Snatching," *A Word with You* #4123, *www.gospelcom.net.*

4. Wesley Duewel, *Mighty Prevailing Prayer* (Grand Rapids, Mich.: Zondervan, 1990), 152.

5. Mrs. Charles E. Cowman, *Streams in the Desert* (Grand Rapids Mich.: Zondervan, 1925), 314–15.

6. Christenson, *What Happens When Women Pray*, 32.

Appendix: Prayer Lists and Prayer Sheets

1. Evelyn Christenson, *A Study Guide for Evangelism Praying* (St. Paul, Minn.: 1992).

Recommended Reading

Prayer, General

Discovering How to Pray, Hope MacDonald, Zondervan 1976
Pray, How to Be Effective in Prayer, Warren Myers, NavPress 1983
Prayer, Conversing with God, Rosalind Rinker, Zondervan 1959
The Hour That Changes the World, Dick Eastman, Baker 1978
The Power of Prayer in a Believer's Life, Charles H. Spurgeon, Emerald 1993
What Happens When Women Pray, Evelyn Christenson, Victor 1975
With Christ in the School of Prayer, Andrew Murray, Revell 1953
Talking with My Father, Ray Stedman, Discovery House 1997
The Power of Personal Prayer, Jonathan Graf, NavPress 2002

Prayer, Warfare

Battling the Prince of Darkness, Evelyn Christenson, Victor 1990
Prayer Is Invading the Impossible, Jack Hayford, Logos International 1977

Praise

To Know Him by Name, Kay Arthur, Multnomah 1995
Behold Your God, Myrna Alexander, Zondervan 1978
The Attributes of God, Arthur W. Pink, Baker 1975
The Knowledge of the Holy, A.W. Tozer, Harper & Row 1961

Confession

The Bondage Breaker, Neil T. Anderson, Harvest House 1990
The Calvary Road, Roy Hession, Christian Literature Crusade (no date)
Brokenness: The Heart God Revives, Nancy Leigh DeMoss, Moody 2002

Marriage

The Christian Family, Larry Christenson, Bethany 1970

Two Hearts Praying as One, Dennis and Barbara Rainey, Multnomah 2002

For Moms

When Mothers Pray, Cheri Fuller, Multnomah 1997

Every Day I Pray for My Teenager, Eastman Curtis, Creation House 1996

Praying Scriptures for Your Children, Jodie Berndt, Zondervan 2001

A Mother's Heart, Jean Fleming, NavPress 1982

Inspirational/Devotional

Still Life, Mary Jenson, Multnomah 1997

He Restores My Soul, Jennifer Kennedy Dean, Broadman & Holman 1999

Fresh Wind, Fresh Fire, Jim Cymbala, Zondervan 1997

God Works the Night Shift, Ron Mehl, Multnomah 1994

Streams in the Desert, Mrs. Charles E. Cowman, Zondervan 1925

A Note from Fern Nichols about Moms In Touch International

Let me encourage you to join with other moms who are praying for their children through Moms In Touch International. I'm going to borrow Patrick Henry's words he used when he urged his fellow Virginians to join the Revolution of 1775. "Our brethren [and sisters] are already in the field! Why stand we here idle?" Won't you experience firsthand what happens when moms unite in prayer?

To find out about Moms In Touch International in your area, to obtain information on starting a group, or simply to learn more about the Four Steps of Prayer that make the Moms In Touch hour of prayer so powerful, contact:

Moms In Touch International
P.O. Box 1120
Poway, California 92074–1120
(858) 486–4065
E-mail address: info@MomsInTouch.org
Web site: *www.MomsInTouch.org*

The purpose of Moms In Touch International is to encourage mothers and others to meet and to pray regularly for children and schools. The vision is that every school in the world would be covered in prayer. God is raising up moms worldwide to pray because every child needs a praying mom.

We want to hear from you. Please send your comments about this book to us in care of zreview@zondervan.com. Thank you.

GRAND RAPIDS, MICHIGAN 49530 USA

WWW.ZONDERVAN.COM